AF480726

A Hopeless Dawn

A Hopeless Dawn

BOOK I OF THE
HOPELESS DAWN SERIES

Jill George

AUTHOR OF ILLUMINATING
DARWIN: ARABELLA'S LIGHT

Heinze Quill Publishing

Dedicated to resilient women everywhere, and with particularly heartfelt thanks to Jennifer, Robin, Kathleen, and Patricia—my companions from the very start, my steady support throughout, and my enduring allies today.

Table of Contents

"Being as mean, dirty, tumultuous place as can well be conceived, therefore, a refuge for all tag, rag and bobtail from all quarters and without the least control or government, the streets narrow and filthy as almost to render them impassable in the time of wet weather."

"To witness a gale of wind here baffle almost description…"

The sky is dark, the rain descends.
In torrents from on high
The winds with huffing bursting gusts
Proclaim the storm is nigh.

The flowing waves with fury beat
Against the stubborn rocks.
The wind them hurls it up on high
Against the cliff it smacks.

The sea bards wild and screaming voice
Is heard along the shore.
Seeking its high and rocky nest
Amid the dismal roar.

The lightning flashes from the sky
In forked flakes it darts.
The thunders awful rumbling noise
Strikes terrors to the heart.

The refoils are now tossed about
Whom the wanton wave
Each sailor with fate affright
Expect a watery grave.

Then who is he who caused this storm
Thus awfully arrived
Who guides the lightning from an ear
The thunders thus to hear.

The God who lives above the sky
Who made this storm it is.
He made the heavens, earth and sky
And all that in them is.

JOHN WATTS TREVAN, *A SUMMARY OF MEMOIRS OF THE
PARISH OF ST. ENDELLION PRIOR TO THE YEAR 1834*

Foreword

In 1888, in the quietude of an art studio in a thatched cottage, nestled at the corner of Rue des Beaux Arts at number 19 Mackensie in the serene fishing village of Newlyn, Cornwall, Frank Bramley used an innovative square brush technique to weave tales of the heart and soul. With each stroke, he captured the essence of life in this rugged, cliff-strewn landscape, the human spirit's resilience in the face of adversity, and the tender moments that have endured across the ages. His paintings from the Newlyn School transport us to a world where time moves gently, revealing stories of love, longing, and the eternal struggle against life's relentless and ever-changing winds and tides.

Praised by the Royal Academy after having been purchased for the nation by the Chantrey Bequest, *A Hopeless Dawn* is one of Bramley's most favored works. Penlee House has said, "The painting's strong emotional and narrative content, together with its aesthetic appeal and tonal harmony, make this one of the most admired Newlyn School works to this day."

As I stood before *A Hopeless Dawn*, the masterpiece that ignited my fascination at the Tate London, I felt an ineffable connection to the people portrayed. Their characterizations became etched into my mind and stained my heart with the raw emotions of the brutality of their existence. It was here, amid a busy day at the Tate, that seeds of an idea instantly took root and gripped me to the core—to breathe life into these characters, to give them a voice and to let their stories unfold like the strong Cornish legends that have endured over time.

While many will see a grief-stricken woman in the painting, bereft from loss, I see more. In fact, the young woman in the painting was a real woman named Effy Reynolds James. Who was she beyond a beautiful model for this sorrowful painting? We likely will never know. However, I know the women of Cornwall were strong throughout history and so I longed to tell the story of a woman who clung to strength and determination in her lowest hours. In my story, the women in the painting figure out how to keep going, despite all that is thrown against them from nature, man, and society. In my story, these women, these very strong women, use their wit and grit to continue to make a life for themselves and those around them and you will see how they accomplish this as you turn these pages.

These initial roots, the first beginnings of the story, have grown into what will be a series of novels that seek to be a tribute, a continuation, and an exploration: a tribute to the genius of Bramley and the Newlyn School, who crafted such poignant narratives on canvas but speak to me as live characters in my mind; a continuation of the lives lived behind those soulful eyes, waiting for their stories to be told and appreciated even more fully; and an exploration into the depths of the strength of human experience, where love and loss, dreams, superstitions, and despair, are the tumultuous tides that shape our existence as always.

In the pages of the several novels in the series, you will embark on journeys through time and place, guided by the brushstrokes of history recorded by Frank Bramley. Through his works that will include *Everyone His Own Tale, For Such Is The Kingdom of Heaven, Delicious Solitude*, and *When Blue Evening Slowly Falls*, you will see people's daily lives and walk the cobbled streets and dirt paths of Port Quin, Port Isaac, London, and Falmouth, feeling the salt-laden misty breeze on your skin. You will witness the enduring human spirit and run up against the superstitions that are Cornish legend.

These stories have been created as an ode to the indomitable intelligence and human spirit of the people of Cornwall as well as the timeless artistry of Frank Bramley. They are an invitation to immerse yourself in the lives of characters who, though born of paint and canvas, resonate with the very essence of our shared humanity as Frank Bramley meant them to be.

May this novel series transport you to a world based on light and goodness, where every dawn, even the most hopeless, carries the promise of new beginnings.

With heartfelt appreciation.

– JILL GEORGE

Preface

The essence of a good historical fiction thriller lies in the interweaving of fact, fiction, and suspense—a set of brush strokes that weaves spells, each with its own texture, colour and depth. The tale that I hope will grip you today will bring you into the maritime realm of Port Quin, a setting that is drenched in ancient legends and traditions and is the throbbing heart of our narrative.

Many have found themselves held captive by the soul-stirring painting *A Hopeless Dawn*, that Cornish locals and guides refer to as a visual tribute to the legend of a mighty storm that sadly sunk a fishing fleet in 1841, rendering the bustling town of Port Quin a desolate slip of rocks. The pathos etched into every "block style" brush stroke of Frank Bramley's painting captures the palpable despair of a young woman, and what must have certainly been an entire community, abruptly torn apart by the relentless forces of nature. In fact, the census of 1841 details about one hundred lives in Port Quin; but there were almost none ten years later in 1851.

However, a keen observer might notice a subtle controversy quietly simmering beneath the surface of this common narrative. The skeptics among us, perhaps relying on their reverence for empirical evidence, adamantly assert that it was the unyielding march of progress and the cruel waning of the Pilchard supplies, rather than the wrath of a storm, that led to Port Quin's untimely demise. This logical perspective is based in connecting facts together but fails to accommodate the complexity and multilayered nature of history.

For the narrative is written in the misty realms of yesteryears where we find our most intriguing revelations. Two manuscripts alluded to by current local historians and penned by brothers Dr. Frederick Trevan, a surgeon trained at St. Bartholomew's in London, in 1833-1834, and John Watts Trevan of Port Isaac, also in 1834, shine a different light on the tales that had been told for centuries. Dr Trevan's piece *The History of Port Isaac and Port Quin*, the typescript held by the Cornish Studies Library at Kresen Kernow (the Cornwall Centre) in Redruth, meticulously documented the residents of Port Isaac, Port Quin, and the surrounding areas, and mentions a vital piece of information—a storm that indeed obliterated a herring fleet back in 1697, leaving a heart rendering legacy of twenty widows. John Watts Trevan's over three-hundred-page book, complete with coloured pencil drawings of estates and churches that his brother's work does not include, adds a bit more detail to the tragic story of 1697. How these brothers know about this story they don't say. Could the story have been passed down from their grandfather, a merchant and then their father, a customs officer? John Watts Trevan's account appears below.

"Port Quin is a very amicant, romantic cove and village and
in former times the most populous place in this parish.

Great numbers of sea faring people residing (were) here, but in the year 1697 a most disastrous occurrence happened to the poor fishermen who been up into Port Isaac bay one night on the herring fishery where caught in a gale of wind at N. W. and not being able to beat down against it, they almost all perished and it is said that more than twenty widows were left in Port Quin in consequence of this unfortunate catastrophe. After this the village went greatly to decay—the greater part of the seafaring inhabitants removed to Port Isaac convincing it to be more adapted for their fishing operations. All the houses in Port Quin on the Endellion side except two or three belong to McSuy of Roscarrock. The following are the housekeepers with their number to family now residing here" (pages 294 – 296). He then lists sixteen families with seventy-five people in the families' total in subsequent detail.

Why did the brothers choose to write about this particular story in addition to several other specific stories they included in their books? Is it possible then that the legend is not simply a quaint tale, spun for the amusement of holidaymakers? Can it be that the tale is not a complete fabrication but something commonly known? Might the echoes of this early catastrophe have woven themselves into the tapestry of the local folklore, eventually being attributed to an event that occurred well over a century later? Could the storm of 1697 be the ghost of the pain still felt through the centuries, a lost truth masked by the cold fact of dwindling supplies and the relentless march of progress? These two literate and bright brothers documented many elements of life in St. Enbellion Parish with numbers and illustrations and likely believed the story to be true in order to include it with the other forms of documentation.

Therefore, while additional research is desirable and required, in part at least, the questions posed here can be answered with some form of a 'yes.'

We do know of a similar situation that seems oddly like the Port Quin story; therefore, lending it possible legitimacy. Sadly, telegrams and letters documented that on October 14, 1881, in the Berwickshire port of Eyemouth in Scottland, 189 seamen were lost in a storm that came up while the fishing fleet was out at sea directly in front of the village. Apparently in that storm, only one boat out of twenty returned two days later. Hundreds of fatherless children were left as a result. An incredible memorial of each family impacted was sculpted in 2016 by Jill Watson and bronzed as a tribute to the strength of the women who carried on with their families despite their losses.

In the pages that follow, I delve deeper into this intriguing interplay of fact and fable, an amalgam of reality, myth, and imagination that paints a layered narrative with the known facts of 1841, as the painting *A Hopeless Dawn* itself. This novel is not just an exploration, but an invitation to navigate the corridors of history, to challenge the accepted truths, and to unveil the captivating power of narratives that have survived all these years and all the stories that followed it.

Within this literary journey, I will unearth the shards of the past, piece them together, and dare to look upon the face of history, acknowledging that often, fact and fiction are frustratingly two sides of the same, weathered coin.

Welcome, then, to an adventure that transcends time and challenges what we think is reality via a gothic romance based on a painting, which is itself based on legends and facts that are compellingly interconnected. Your journey into the depths of Cornwall's Port Quin's legends begins here.

– JILL GEORGE

The Fish

Small and seemingly insignificant as individuals but mighty in numbers, these scaly, glassy eyed, gaping mouthed swimmers have outwitted man for centuries. Villagers in Port Quin and Port Isaac, along with hundreds of other Cornish coastal towns, devoted each day to the ancient and sacred pursuit of the understanding and capture of these elusive, hidden creatures, the silvery lifeblood of their very existence.

Fishing was no mere occupation, but a vocation that demanded every ounce of brain power and physical strength that men, women, and children had. Countless hours, heaped upon hours, immeasurable in their passing, were spent in the ceaseless study of the sea's hidden swimmers and their capture. In his book *A Summary of Memoirs of the Parish of St. Endellion Prior to the Year 1834*, John Watts Trevan details the kinds of fish that were the fishermen's elusive adversaries and the collective knowledge of what time of year they could be found. He states,

> "Whales are not unfrequently saw here…grampus (a large dolphin or orca) in the autumn, sharks at all times of year and of extraordinary size…rays, porpus…monk…sunfish…

herring, mackerel, cod and ling from Christmas to Ladyday, congar most times of year but most numerous in spring, turbot, a scarce fish caught in the sun of summer, about twenty years since they were plentiful and cheap…and pilchards, the most important fish of all…come in August."

From watching birds find the best fishing spots to looking for ripples in surface waters, fisherman studied and honed their craft. Testing baits, nets and lures, seamen discovered new methods to catch pilchards, sometimes referred to as "the silver darlings," in huge batches with boats formed in a circle and nets latched to boats, scooping the unsuspecting school en masse. Fishermen became scholars of the sea, reading its winds and moods based on ancient wisdom and the habits of the fish based on their prey's habits, which was as elusive as the sea itself.

Baked in the sun by day and pouring over charts by dim fish oil lamps at night, grizzled fishermen spoke of tales of the deep, seeking to find "thick" catches for their future purses. They compared currents and undercurrents, shoals and hidden coves, and times and seasons when the fish would be plenty or scarce and how to prepare their weather-beaten boats.

The women, too, were a part of this unyielding way of life. Their sinewy arms hauled huge baskets of fish with a thick band wrapped around the fish basket and their heads to the fish barrels on shore. Their hands mended nets and fishermen's wounded minds and hearts. They understood the language and timing of the sea and most important of all, how to wait. Their lives were in a long, perpetual dance with fish, and all they held dear rested on these little aquatic mice. For every day was the relentless set up, clean, net mind, haul, "cat and mouse" game all in the name of fish.

And the fish, in their shimmering silver tide, were clever keepers of the deep, eluding capture with almost omniscient skill. Despite the trickery of the nets and boats, the fish still had their day in the untamed sea. However, as the years trudged on, the iron wheels of the railways laid tracks on the land and more and more hungry mouths demanded the harvest of the sea. As humanity swelled, the once-abundant fish dwindled. The plentiful waters grew sparse and fishing efforts became "thin." Fish scattered beneath the waves, driven to distant and deeper realms by the relentless pursuit of nets and lines like never before. Always mysterious, the fickle sea and its darlings, the fish, those that remained at least, fled man once more, and had won again.

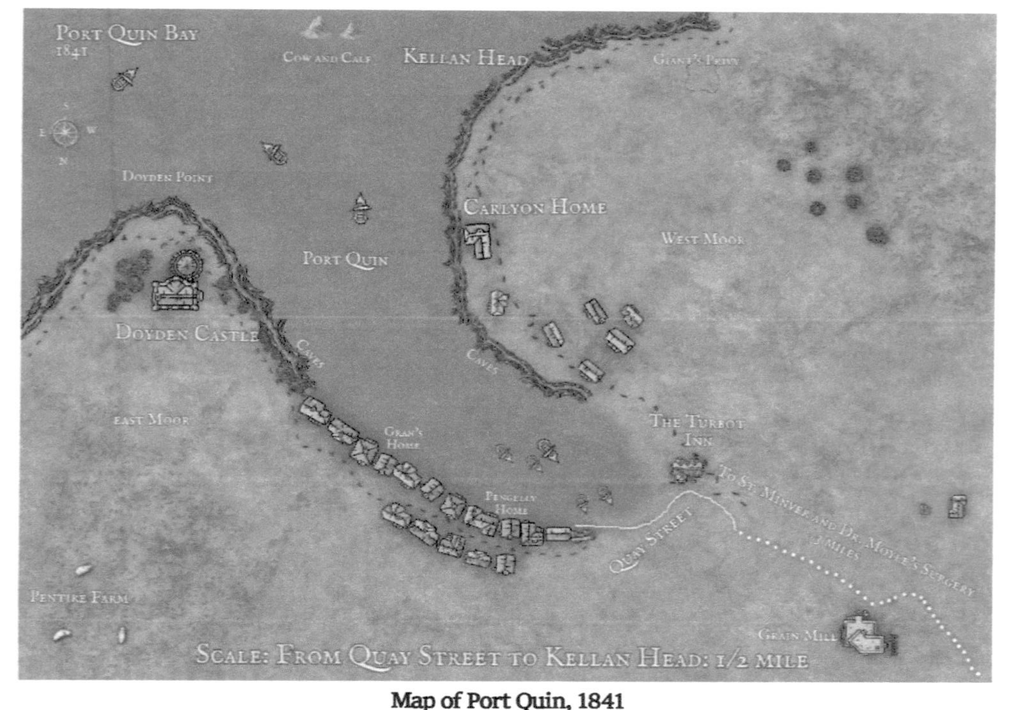

Map of Port Quin, 1841

Created for A Hopeless Dawn *and illustrated by Jill George*

Chapter One

THE STORY I TELL MYSELF

PORT QUIN, CORNWALL, U.K.

AUGUST 30, 1841

My heart was heavy as I looked down from the road to the quay, once lined on both sides with boats, cargoes, and crews, but now becoming barren. The grey stone and red brick cottages surrounding it stood either empty or in the process of becoming empty and my mind struggled as it compared today's harsh reality with the ebullient activity of the harbour's yesterdays.

I walked from the road to the heart of Quay Street. "The tide shall continue its endless ebb and flow, and the flowers shall bloom in their season, and stars shall shine their brilliant light upon the world," I whispered, my voice choking. "But for me, the womb that was once Port Quin is becoming shattered, and I am unable to bear watching it become empty."

Where once a hundred villagers of all ages had prospered

in a couple of dozen houses, now only melancholy voices filled the air. The enormity of the tragedy bore down on me like the massive waves that had caused this desolation to begin with. What had been my neighbors' homes—the Guys and the LaCombes, among others who were lost—were of course abandoned. The wind whistled mournfully through the open windows of several homes and doors creaked and gently rapped open and shut in the breeze. When I reached the very cottage where I had grown up, I had hoped to feel some solace, a respite from the torment that plagued my mind and soul. But instead, the anguish that had been haunting me for days seemed to grow stronger in this desolate place, suffocating me with its cruel crushing force.

The desolation was one thing. What I had done on top of that was another thing altogether. The weight of the guilt over what I had done, and failed to do, never left my mind, not for a minute, and never would entirely. My lack of action to warn the others. And how I had betrayed someone who had loved me completely and fiercely was a sin. Would I ever come to live with myself after these things I had done? Would God forgive me?

The small waves in the cove crashed against the rocky black shore in a relentless rhythm, a reminder of the unforgiving and powerful nature of the world. The putrid smell of decaying seaweed filled my nostrils. The fish cellars stood gaping open like mouths waiting to be filled.

The path made of small stones just past the Turbot Inn crunched beneath my boots and as I walked up the slope towards Kellan Head, my breath became heavier. Over my left shoulder, the sea jeered at me, as if to say, "I know what you did." The endless blue expanse was a reminder of the vastness of the world and the harm it was capable of, which was equal to what I was capable of, even in my own insignificance. Despite being overwhelmed by the enormity of it all, I couldn't help but feel drawn to the sea's fierce power, its unyielding strength, and startling beauty, a reflection of my own determination to face my inner demons, confront my decisions, and make amends with the rough, brutal world. More than one wreck, literal or otherwise, had taken place on these rocks—and I was the only one to survive both.

I trudged up the slope to the right of the quay, passing smugglers' caves and hideouts that I had used myself over the years. I ventured uphill all the way to Kellan Head, which was the special place that William, my heart's desire, and I cherished. I stopped for a moment to catch my breath. Far in the distance, the rocks named the Cow and Calf stared back at me with their rocky brown faces. I decided that I had a choice to make, and I needed to make it now: Either let the demons eat away at me or find another way to live.

So, I reached the top of the Head, which was glorious in every type of weather; I had come to let it inspire me. Today, the rugged cliffs below were lashed by the strong sea wind, which howled and moaned. I was entranced by the turbulent spectacle that splashed and whirled below me. The waves crashed against the rocks, the white frothy foam spraying high into the air, as though a giant beast was breathing heavily upon the shore. *Oh, if that beast could only tell me what to do,* I thought to myself.

From my vantage point atop the cliff, the bay stretched out before me like a vast, black canvas, the same sight the fishermen would have seen for the last time before they died. The wind whipped at my calico bonnet and flung my skirt about my legs. As the wind intensified, I smelled the salty tang of the sea mixed with the scent of seaweed and mussels clinging to the rocks below. Port Quin itself, wedged in between two cliffs, possessed an otherworldly charm, its narrow shape, a slender crescent of water, seemed to also cling precariously to the edge of the sea, just like a mussel. The ruggedness of the terrain echoed in the contours of the village, with its small, weathered cottages huddled together for solace against the ceaseless winds. The slate roofs, blackened by time, appeared like grave-stones marking the passage of countless lives, each brick and stone etched with tales of triumph and tragedy.

The raucous sounds of the gulls calling to each other, the wind and the waves grew more intense, as if the elements were beginning a battle and I was caught in the middle of it. Another storm was approaching. The clouds roiled and churned, creating a sense of uncertainty, blocking the sunlight. On the edge of the precipice of the Head, I could have been swept away by the elements at any moment like many before me.

Many minutes passed. Caught up in the power of the sea and wind, and in their wild, darkening majesty, I decided to make a vow to the sea and those buried within it. I owed them that much, despite their abuses of me, my mother, and many of the women in the village, come to think of it. I would not succumb to the pain of the past and live whatever remained of life as if dead inside. "I, Effy Pengelly, vow to no longer mourn over what was lost and the part I played, but to harness you, demons, for good, to build a renewed strength to carry on, in defiance of the forces of nature that sought to tear everything apart," I cried. "Do you hear me?" I screamed, shaking my fist at the wild wind off Quin's Bay. I would face down whatever gale in life that came with the power within me. But first I would have to tell the truth of my story—to myself if no one else.

Chapter Two

A SENSE OF FOREBODING

PORT QUIN, CORNWALL, U.K.

AUGUST 2, 1841

As the sun tried to creep out through the slate-coloured gauzy stretch of clouds that threatened rain, small sea pinks, one of my favorite flowers, and yellow mounds of gorse dotted the vast grumbling moors. We humble parishioners—mostly seamen, miners, farmers, and families dressed in our meager Sunday best—trudged up the muddy three-and-a-half-mile path to the ancient and disintegrating gray stone church of St. Minver's. We gathered, exhausted as we were from our week's labour, for the christening of the shoemaker, Mr. Buller's son. The tall conical spire with a small cross on top glowered down at us and the unpresuming, crooked gravestones below.

Each person had his or her own reasons for coming to church, whether it was for the love of the Lord or simply to be seen by those who loved the Lord. As several men and women approached the entrance of the church, Caden Bolitho, a strong young fisherman, was leaning on a pillar, a blade of grass between his teeth, lingering, greeting each church goer with a warm and welcoming smile. As my mother Mary and I approached, arm in arm, our long, light summer dresses swishing in the grass, he tossed the blade of grass on the ground and tipped his hat gallantly.

"Good day to ye, Caden," Mother said. "You be looking as handsome as ever."

Caden's gaze shifted quickly from Mother to me with appreciation. I had been his childhood friend since as long as I could remember. Recently, he had been asking for more than mere friendship. He made his intentions toward me quite clear in his frequent requests for walks to and from our Methodist Chapel or the longer walk for special events to church, like today, something my mother was against. Something about Caden wore her the wrong way. "Even though you are both well into marrying age, he's impatient to grow up," Mother often said of him. "An' somethin' 'bout him bothers me. He's too handsome for his own good. I knows what I says."

"Good morning, Mrs. Pengelly," he replied. "And thank you for the kind words," he purred back at her.

"And mind that you don't look at my daughter so," she scoffed, wagging her finger to and fro. "Effy ain't a roast chicken to be drooled over!"

"Definitely not! But she's the most beautiful woman in the Parish, an that's for sartin," Caden said in a low tone, his eyes piercing into mine.

He had always described me as "a classic, regal" beauty with my straight nose and sharp jaw line. My soft blue eyes drew him in, he once poetically mentioned, like the most magical, clear wading pool—and held on to him with a force stronger than that in any metal. I believe I laughed in response. But he enjoyed giving me extravagant compliments. My thick wavy red hair, unusual as it was, seemed to Cade, as rays of the sun at dusk. I was thin but keenly well rounded for a man's eye, as he often said of me. Yet his descriptions of me, while generous, often annoyed me.

I supposed a person's beauty was a form of wealth to some; but with our meager means, little good it did me or mine. None of his flattery really mattered in my way of thinking. To me, beauty, true beauty, was what was inside a person that gave a person grit, like the cliffs or a colour that shone from within, like the sea that had the ability to shift it colours in the sun. The cliffs, the sea, and the sun were magical and enduring. They were to be admired. Nothing changed their strength and beauty, which could be relied on as a constant. They had always been here and they would always exist.

My cheeks grew hot at their words, but I couldn't help but smile at Caden's casual chortle as he dropped his gaze and stood more respectfully, at full height, as we walked by. He knew Mother well and most likely thought his presence at the christening would speak well of him given her Christian devotion.

"Mother!" I scolded, gently shaking Mother's arm before turning to Caden. "Mornin', Cade."

I met Cade's eyes as we passed, and in that moment, time seemed to stand still. The world around us faded back to childhood games of "over the cliff," where we would pretend to jump dramatically over a precipice, only to land safely a few feet below on a ledge. I was twenty and he was twenty-two now, but I remembered the times when we were eight and ten like they were yesterday. Sweet scents of the heather on the moors and local farms reminded me of our deep and unbreakable bond.

As Cade followed us up the steps and into the church, I could feel his eyes burn on my backside like the August sun. He had told me many times he thought me the most beautiful girl he had ever seen. That the combination of my red hair and deep blue eyes had a magical quality he more than admired. I appeared to be his first choice as a possible wife. Yet as strong as my feelings were for him, I wasn't completely settled on him as a match. And that lack of decision was causing tension to build up between us.

Why wasn't I settled? To be honest, I was distracted by thoughts and feelings about someone else other than Cade. And that someone else was in the church that day as well. The tension between Cade and I built day by day because he was in tune with this changeable feeling of mine towards him. I swore Cade could tell when I was put off by him in the slightest way, even though I tried to hide it. He could read me like we would read the leaves of trees turning over in the wind when a storm was approaching. And I often felt myself to be in conflict. Was it possible to have some strong feelings for Cade on the one hand, but to grow fond of someone else as well?

I sat in between my parents in the unyielding embrace of the wooden pew, transfixed on the austere form of Parson Hockings, a tall, thin man whose harsh appearance matched the harshness of his sermons. Above his surplice, Parson Hockings' Adam's apple, sharp and pointed, bounded up and down with each syllable he uttered from the ornate pulpit. As he went on and on, we, his congregation, were engulfed in sweltering heat, the thick suffocating air barely lightened by the open door. Everyone fanned themselves as best they could, their brows slick with sweat, desperate for relief. Pungent body odour wafted through the air despite our best attempts to contain it. The pews groaned with the weight of restless bodies, shifting in discomfort, eager for the sermon to end. As the pale rays of a summer morning streamed through the stained-glass windows, they illuminated the dark slate floor in patterned patches of light.

Parson Hockings preached about the sanctity of the sacrament of baptism, but more about the sanctity of marriage and its purpose. His words were a clear warning to the young women in the congregation. My face grew hot as he spoke, my heart raced with a mix of fear and longing all the same. Why would Parson Hockings stress marriage to the point of precisely emphasizing the reason for marriage in the first place, to prevent fornication? *Because to stress that point was causing everyone to be thinking exactly that now*, I thought to myself.

This led me to wonder exactly what the people in the church were thinking about. Were they all seriously considering his sermon? I imagined that some of the local fishermen, Mr. Tremaine, Mr. Hicks, Mr. Tamlyn and Mr. Collins, those that made it here, tanned and cracked from the sun, were thinking more about sleep, food, or drink. That was what my brothers, Richard, and Taran, would have thought about if they were here, which they were not. My older brothers, farm labourers who sometimes also fished, lived far up the road on

Roscarrock farm. They had given up mining at the Port Quin and the Gilson Cove mines this year for work above grass. Most likely they were still asleep from too much ale from the adventures of the previous night at one inn or another. My friends, Kensa and Melwynn, those pious, hardworking girls, Kensa hauling fish baskets and Melly working at the Turbot Inn, sitting at the back of the church, would be listening to the sermon, and thinking about the warning, like I was. The women of the village smugly acknowledged the importance of the warning, for they had firsthand experience with the act itself and its consequences. And the men? The men of the village, like my father, paid it little mind at all. Parson Hockings had much work to do here, and I took it that he looked out over a sea of bored and distracted faces, the poor man.

My musings wandered further. What did a certain hay coloured head a few rows ahead of me, the object of my thoughts, William Carlyon, think about that sermon? William had moved to Port Quin less than a year ago from north Cornwall, and his family had a reputation for being pirates and smugglers. Why they had this reputation I was not exactly sure, except that anyone that was from farther than two or three miles away was considered a foreigner and not to be trusted.

I admired William's unusual appearance for a Cornish young man, with his tall frame and sandy coloured hair and dark green eyes rather than the more common dark hair, dark eyes, and stocky build which was Cade's appearance. William sat patiently and calmly listening as the Parson lashed out at those who would be likely to break God's covenants. With difficulty, I tried to refocus on the Parson's booming voice as it filled the small space. But, in truth, it was William who filled the space in my heart with hope and longing for all that was good in life. Perhaps if I tarried at the door or at the end of my pew I could run into him and gain the favor of a few words after church. He and I had spoken together here at church and at the quay several times, and I had grown more than fond of him.

My mind wandered back to the first time I had met William and his family when they arrived in Port Quin in their new horse-drawn wagon. No one in Port Quin owned a wagon, so I am sure I stared at them in some awe as they rolled up. Henry, William's younger brother, had attempted to jump out of the wagon but tripped on the edge. He landed badly on a stone wall, wounding his knee. The wound bled out quickly, but luckily I was on my way to the Doctor's surgery with bandages in my basket. I remember William's father telling Henry to get back in the wagon and they would be on their way after gathering the things that they needed. But I insisted that I clean and dress the wound. "I can see the fat layer through the puncture. Likely it will become inflamed. Given how much it is bleeding out, we should press wet tea on it to stop the blood from flowing. Best to clean and bandage this now," I had said forcefully to Charles Carlyon, William's father, looking back. William held on to Henry during the cleaning and bandaging as Henry squirmed and yelped in pain. I recall thinking I had never seen such a handsome man as William. Or such a calm and caring brother. We had made a connection somehow from that very first meeting. What kind of connection I could not say exactly.

I shifted in the pew, restless but trying to stay still. William possessed the kind of rugged alure that was like the sun shining on the depths of an ancient cave's forgotten passage, inviting those who gazed upon it to plunge into a world of enchantment. He had a bubbling nature that lurked underneath his composed and calm exterior. I considered his eyes to add a kind of angelic look to his face that contrasted with his disheveled, curly hair that seemed to hint at his enthusiastic spirit that defied the conventions of society. His large hands appeared to have the strength and ability to tear a man apart but I had only seen them use the most graceful of motions.

As the sermon continued, Cade looked round at me from his seat several pews in front, trying to catch my eye. I averted my gaze and felt a shiver run down my spine. I was sure I knew what he was thinking, and it wasn't about the sanctity of marriage or any hymn. Caden had a compelling, confident way about him. A slow-moving prowl that made me feel special, wanted, pursued, and hunted. His manner of speech had something of a gentle air about it, probably because in addition to being a fisherman, he also worked in the Turbot Inn and was used to mixing with all sorts of people. Even though he couldn't read, Cade acquired knowledge and learned in both a streetwise and lofty manner. He could converse with anyone, be it fisherman or gentleman, even though he came from as humble means as the rest of us: his father long lost at sea and his mother and three sisters all fish haulers. But he also had a wild, feral side and today, as the subject of the sermon unfolded, he made me uneasy.

Cade, in contrast to William, had a melancholic allure about him, a tragic, romantic edge that seemed to have etched its mark upon his face and soul. When Cade looked at me, his presence was not only captivating, but I was drawn to him like a moth to a flame. Beneath his shadowy façade, he had a tenderness, a gentleness, that he reserved for those who had earned his trust. In my company, his stormy eyes softened, revealing the needs that few were allowed to see. His deep and resonant voice had the power to soothe or ignite, and his face was laced with intensity.

Thankfully, Mother was sitting next to my left, her eyes closed in prayer, and I took comfort in her calmness, now and always. Her soft brown curls pulled back neatly in her bonnet, Mother was a devout Methodist, a hard-working dawn to dusk spinner, seamstress, mender, wife, and mother who had lost three children after me and one before. Mother was no stranger to the hard life at Port Quin. I knew that she took the side of the Lord's and Parson Hocking's words completely.

Father, sitting on my right, was a contributor to the hardships we faced. Why he was here at all at the church today, as he wasn't usually in attendance? He was sitting particularly close to Cornelia, that tawny haired, pretty but sullen, buxom grain miller's daughter, younger than me. *No wonder he is here. He seemed to like the buxom ones. The shame of it. No doubt he disregarded the parson's words completely during the sermon as he did at home. Poor Mother!*

My father. The brilliant Jago Pengelly. I turned to gaze only for a second at his haggard profile as the beauty of St. Minver's contrasted completely in the background like righteous versus evil. He had left schooling at fourteen like most boys to pursue his calling at sea. As he told it, his time at school was spent learning how to make and repair nets, which he passed down to Mother and me. He was considered an educated man who could read a chart or map and sometimes, when he wanted to, taught others seamanship.

He was an excellent navigator and knot tyer. He could find fish by watching birds. Of course, he had his favorite spots, like the one off of Castle Rock, near Port Gavern. He could have been a leader of men in town but he was too greedy with his own talents for that. He was always lusting after women. A tyrant at home, he was often verbally and even physically abusive. Taciturn. Not good with children. My mother would never go against her wedding vows and leave him, but I often wished she would. In short, he was a force I avoided, if possible.

As I sat there, surveying the minds and thoughts of those around me, a sharp, painful sense of foreboding began to creep over me, as if the decaying church itself was trying to tell me something. I felt as well as heard voices, low and grumbling, echoing in my mind. My grandmother Elizabeth, who was my namesake and known to be familiar with the "dark arts" referred to these kinds of thoughts or feelings as omens when she experienced them. I wondered at times if I too possessed the dark arts as I had, on occasion, had some odd premonitions of insignificant events before they happened. I had tossed these thoughts aside in the past, as meaningless, as my mother said they were. My grandmother said they were a gift that I should learn more about in time but my mother frowned on these conversations.

But now I more clearly than ever before had the sense that there was someone or something calling out to me, and it seemed as if they were leaving or dying. The sound was a low, deep throated groan of sorts that was impossible to ignore and difficult to decipher. I wasn't sure if I was actually hearing something or merely having thoughts in my mind coming from people who had been here centuries before me, who sat in the same spot I did, in a crowd of parishioners not dissimilar from mine.

I looked around to see if anyone else was hearing what I heard or noticed my reaction to what I heard. No one seemed to notice. I tried to focus on my surroundings instead of these unnerving sounds which caused an aching in my mind and heart. My eyes roamed around the interior of the church as I gaped around the interior of the church. The space was dimly lit, and the sunlight sifted in through the stained-glass windows, casting a colorful glow on the stone walls. The pulpit was made of dark wood, with intricate patterns and designs carved into its surface. I noticed several black, jagged cracks in the slate floor.

All at once, the cracks in the floor opened, slowly at first and then they burst wide open. They loomed before me as large as graves. Inside were the greyish white bones of those who had died long ago. Bones lay in heaps, with arms and legs tangled and jaws open. Black eye sockets stared back at me. Shocked, I felt like I might gag as I drew in my breath. I began to feel extremely cold despite the heat inside of the church. The heart ache and longing I felt grew more intense, as if someone close to me had just died unexpectedly. Within me, I had a painful feeling of being lost, utterly lost. I felt as if a hole inside me opened that could never be refilled. I shuddered. Tears sprang to my eyes and I felt a need to sob uncontrollably. I shivered and hugged my arms about me. I felt very sad, despondent, and isolated even though I was sitting in a crowded church and next to my own mother.

"Praise be to God!" Parson Hocking shouted out loudly, his cue for the congregation to repeat the phrase in his sermon. Instantly, the cracks shrank to normal size and the intensity of the feeling vanished. My tears dried. The tension left and I felt warm again. My throat felt less constricted. The heartache I felt was gone. Whatever the "omen" was had only lasted a few seconds and then vanished. I glanced at Mother in a panic to see if she noticed my discomfort, but she sat, her eyes fixed on Parson Hockings. I sighed with relief. Tall and imposing, the Parson's figure restored my calm as he spoke.

What the omen was I couldn't explain. Deeply confused, I was disturbed and troubled about what had just happened-about the sense I had had of people calling out to me from another place and time, from beyond death. On the one hand, it seemed as if it was some kind of strange message. Could it have been more than an image or feeling, an actual contact from the past? I was nervous yet interested at the same time. Yet, I certainly didn't want this strange world seeping into my life.

I looked beyond the Parson at the altar adorned with candles and a simple white cloth for help. Above the altar hung a large wooden cross, which cast a shadow on the floor below. As I gazed upon these religious symbols, they too held a meaning that was beyond my grasp, and I felt drawn to them, trying to draw from them solace and guidance. As the service continued, I sought comfort from their ancient presence. Maybe whatever I felt was not evil, whatever it had been. I was not alone but accompanied by generations of people who had come before me to this same spot, seeking consolation, meaning and purpose in the vast, unknowable, unexplainable and harsh universe. The harsh existence that was Port Quin. The harsh existence that I often yearned to leave behind me but saw no escape from. But why was I having impressions of their losses, their feelings? I was perplexed and frightened.

Mercifully, the sermon following the baby having had water poured over his sleeping head had ended the service, and we were free to go in peace. The crowd bustled this way and that in a hurry to leave the overheated church. I blinked, still suffused with the intensity of the premonition. Cade tried to nudge his way over towards me with intent. Someone touched my arm from behind, causing me to pause and turn. William looked firmly in my eyes and with his deep voice said, "May I have the pleasure of walking you home?"

"I would be delighted," I replied, as I managed a smile back at him, trying to push down my unease to some deep place inside me.

We passed Cade as we walked past the pew where I sat. William's hand was at the small of my back. Cade's smile had dropped from his face and was replaced with an angry glare. I was too glad to have William's comfort after my ordeal to worry about Cade. I gave him a look as if to say, "It's only a walk, for heaven's sake." But Cade's look in return troubled me. I saw in it a haunted, secret world where heartache and revenge converged. and I wondered anxiously where it would lead.

Chapter Three

The Soft Nature of Dreams

Port Quin, Cornwall, U.K.

August 2, 1841

"That was a pleasant christening and sermon, was it not?" William asked, his eyebrows arched in obvious sarcasm as we left the crumbling steps and ivy-covered walls of the church. He looked quite handsome in his dark blue jacket, tan trousers, and neatly tied cravat. His eyes were full of merriment, and I delighted in his happy, breezy demeanor, which was a welcome relief after my ordeal in the church and contrasted so sharply with my father's harsh, surly tone at home.

"Yes," I laughed. "His focus on marriage had the exact opposite effect on those in attendance, I believe." I pulled a branch out of my way as we crossed over on to the long-beaten path leading towards home.

"God's will versus human nature. Quite a battle for a country parson, don't you think?" William teased. To me, William seemed to possess an unusual manner and an intelligence that I had never encountered before. He connected people's concerns and issues so quickly together, making sense of things before I could even put them into words, much less express them. I glanced at him and in that moment, it was as if I could see his mind working on many things at the same time. I realized then that what I suspected before was true: that he was highly intelligent.

"Indeed. Quite so!" I agreed, fumbling at the awkwardness of the topic. I turned over my shoulder to see if Mother was following behind us, which she was. I also saw Cade further back, laughing and slapping the back of a friend, Jack Rowe, another young fisherman who was a bit black hearted in my book. I was glad to see Cade in a better mood, seemingly unconcerned about my walking with William.

"And what of your nature, Effy? What is it in your nature to do or to be?" William asked sincerely, turning to look at me as we began to walk the three miles back to Quay Street.

"I like spinning, knitting, sewing, and net mending, which is fine work, but I would like to do more with my life. That is, more of my work assisting Dr. Moyle." I worked as Dr. Moyle's assistant for more than two years now when he was in Port Quin at Quin Cottage where he held his surgery two days a week. I helped him in all manner of ways, bandaging wounds, gathering herbs for tonics, dosing those who were ill and more. "I have learned much in the ways of healing," I went on, "and I feel this is a calling for me. My mother says I have a gift." I looked down at the ground, smiling a bit shyly. I never loved talking about myself to other people.

I was pleased, as we spoke, that my speech had been

greatly elevated by working with and copying Dr. Moyle. When I first began working with Dr. Moyle, I said "ain't" and "don't rightly know" just like most people of Port Quin. But now, I never use those words because of Dr. Moyle's constant corrections. And I was glad because William's speech definitely was more elevated than most in Port Quin or Port Isaac for that matter. Why I didn't know.

"You should follow that calling. We need a resident healer in the village," William replied, his voice full of caring. I was pleased he took an interest. Father never did. "I recall how well you bandaged Henry's knee when we first arrived. There is much to be learned to avoid sickness, especially among young children. Henry has been afflicted several times..." William drifted off with a sad look in his eyes.

"Sorry to hear that. And you? What dreams or plans do you have if I may ask?" I looked at him and took full stock of his lips, his eyes, his forehead as he spoke. His lips were full and expressive. When he spoke, his exuberance and confidence drew me in like the full moon pulls in anyone who gazes at it.

"I have a dream of starting my own boat building business. I have built small fishing boats and the like already. The boat I fish with is one of the first I built, and it is very seaworthy..." He continued about the features of his boat, the *Hope*, and his dreams of building larger cargo vessels that would be fully rigged with beam sizes of thus and so and keel lengths of over sixty feet with tonnages over one hundred, all of which was more than impressive—but I had gotten lost in the way his mouth moved, in his strong lips and chin. The way he carried his broad chest and shoulders, taut and upright, conveyed to me his inner determination and passion for boat building, which was like seeing his dream come alive in physical form.

As we continued walking, the path undulated with luscious hedges and wildflowers on either side. To my surprise, he came out of his boat building dreams and said, "I see some lovely pink marsh orchids, just there. Would you like me to pick a few for you?" He strode over to the pasture on the right of the path to the flowers.

"Yes, they are beautiful," I called after him. The other people behind us had drawn closer as he bent over to pick the flowers. Cade and his friends were behind Mother. I could hear Cade laughing loudly now, as if he wanted me to know he was not far behind, watching our every move. Father was nowhere in sight. I smiled at Mother as she passed me and continued walking down the path towards home.

"For you and your mother," William said placing a large bouquet of the long-stemmed pink orchids in my hands, his hands touching mine for a few seconds as he gave them to me. I was impressed again with him that he was not so lost in his own dreams that he forgot about me or what might be my interests. He was not overly self-absorbed like many of the men I had encountered.

"Thank you kindly. We will enjoy these on our supper table," I said, my cheeks hot and my heart pounding.

"Effy, I must ask you directly. Are you and Cade in some kind of understanding? He suggests that you are," William said, hurriedly. I understood his meaning completely.

Alarmed, I said quickly, "No, William. Nothing like that." For a brief second we looked into each other's eyes for the truth and saw it there completely. A bare look of true admiration for the other.

I quickly changed the subject as more people were approaching. "I saw your mother at church today. She is looking well. Is your father still away finding work?" I turned to continue walking, flowers in hand. I hoped to find out more about his family, knowing from his eyes upon mine that his family had no dodgy reputation as my father and others accused them of having.

"Yes, Mother is well, but Father is often away," William said, smiling and then turning away as we continued walking to Quay Street. We came to the beginning of Quay Street with the V shape of the port stretched out before us. William paused to take it in.

"Our world is paused, this Sunday morn," he said quietly.

The scene before us was life holding its breath. All was still and calm as we stood at the basin where the sand was still damp from the retreating tide. The sea air was laden with the mingled scent of brine and seaweed, and very pungent, as the remains of the ebbing tide lay rotting in the heat of the day, between tides, waiting for the water's return.

"A perfect time to see the port's hidden wonders," I added. For before us was the cove, a perfect natural V carved into the chunky, jagged coastline with black caves on either side, beckoning to be explored. "I used to hide in that cave closest to my house," I explained, pointing to the left to the cave.

"You weren't afraid of the dark?" William asked, squinting to see the cave.

"Not in the least." I replied, thinking to myself that whatever lay in the cave was less frightening than what I was trying to escape at the time. I knew places to hide, alright.

"Brave woman!" William exclaimed. I smiled in return.

Up the cliffs to the right was the familiar and welcoming Turbot Inn, the only public house in Port Quin. My friend, Melly, and her father ran the inn, which was closed now but would open later in the day to serve afternoon meals and ale for some in town. As most of the residents of Port Quin were Methodists and didn't partake in spirits, the inn served mostly meals. To me, the Turbot's large red and tan brick structure was a comforting second home. Not as a regular patron but given Melly and her father ran it, I was a welcome visitor to the back door and the kitchen for an occasional slice of buttered bread or saffron bun.

A fleet of over thirty fishing vessels was scattered across the port's surface. The smaller skiffs and lugger boats were nestled closer to the shore. Their painted sides were weathered by countless voyages out to sea, which had worn the paint through the persistent assault of waves and sun. Our fishing fleet ironically resembled a school of fish above the water instead of a school typically viewed below, huddled together in between two large rocks for protection. Further out, the larger ships floated idly, their towering masts reached up to touch the haze, like the spiky back fins of larger fish. I thought to make this analogy to William, but then pulled it back as being too imaginary. I hesitated to describe my inner thoughts to him just yet.

William began walking again and shrugged his shoulders, "A bit serene, given how deserted it is today, but also haunting, don't you agree?" I nodded, admiring his show of imagination, and chided myself for not showing my own as well.

We saw Jack Rowe, Cade's friend, just arriving to loiter by

the inn's entrance; William gave him a short acknowledgement of greeting. Jack was something of a loner and a very rough type with a swarthy look and an angry undercurrent that threatened to come to the surface at any time. I was always polite to Jack, as Cade was friends with him, but I had never wanted to include Jack in our games as children. He had a threatening look about him, as many of the boys in the parish did. That look stayed with him into young adulthood. The scars on his nose and chin told stories about the fights he had gotten into, whose stories were now written on his face. *Probably meeting Cade later*, I thought. *Best be gone from here. The two of them together with William nearby would likely create trouble.* I was thankful that William wanted nothing to do with Jack Rowe

People began to reappear in Quay Street as they returned from St. Minver, mostly interested in returning home to get out of the heat of the day. Ready to meet them was an open-air preacher in the common area, Abraham Bastard of Treligga in St. Teath. He was dressed in black from head to toe and held a Bible. William spotted him and steered me away by the elbow at an angle away from him. "Ah, the sage luminary Abraham Bastard is here to preach, I see. Let's walk away from his ravings."

As the man began, someone peeped out of a window not far off and laughed at the preacher's discourse, waving him off with their hand through the dirty panes.

To that, we heard him reply, "Ah, you may laugh here, you may laugh here below, but take my word, there will be no laughing in heaven."

We continued walking up the road towards my house. "No

laughing in heaven? I thought heaven was a joyous place with no pain," I said, looking up at William. "What do you believe?"

"I believe he breaks the serenity of the day with his nonsense," William replied.

We passed Mr. Buller's shoe repair shop, which was closed, of course. I wondered how he enjoyed the christening and what life was like with his new son. Mr. Buller was a kindly and thick set man who had so much business that he had taken on an apprentice. He and his wife, Sara, lived upstairs in the modest building. I admired his positive attitude when all he had to look forward to all day was to sit on his small three-legged stool surrounded by a load of smelly, broken-down boots, both men's and women's. I was glad that he now had his son to add joy to his life. Yet his shop smelled so bad that I wondered how he could tolerate it. I spent as little time there as possible, so I often only spoke to him at church.

Mother and I had hoped that one of my brothers might be interested in the work, but they both preferred the fields to being inside that reeking shop all day. I could smell the sickly black smell of the grease he used on the boots even through the closed door. I could see the tall men's boots lined up on his work bench in various states of repair through the thick glass windowpanes smudged with dirt. The boots were haunting, I thought, waiting for the heels and toes that would occupy them. I turned to William and blurted out, "What stories those dirty old boots could tell!"

"Yes," he surmised. "Let's see. That one there on the right with the hole in the toe could tell a grand story of how it met the sharp end of a hoe at the farm, I daresay." We laughed at the wearisome, uneventful but comical nature of our existence.

"What will these men do without their boots?" I asked him. "I doubt many people have another pair."

"Borrow a pair from someone," he replied, nodding, "or go without until these are repaired."

Mr. Humphrey Craddock's masonry business was the next two-story building on our left and was made of rough-hewn stones and handmade bricks. William paused by the window to admire the assortment of blackened steel masonry tools—hammers, chisels, trowels, and levels, which were neatly arranged in the front window hinting at the craftmanship within. He cocked his head toward the tools and asked me, "Which do you think is more important, the quality of the tools or the quality of the man?"

"From my experience, I would say the quality of the person," I said, deep in thought. "What would you say?" I enjoyed his calm demeanor combined with his sense of humor. The way he seemed to include me in his thoughts was especially endearing.

He looked at me, thinking for a moment. "Depends on the person," he replied, his hands behind his back as he continued walking. I smiled and looked down at the flowers he had given me. Inwardly, I felt a warm rush to my cheeks and an inexplicable glow of appreciation of his thoughtfulness and insight.

When we finally reached my family's cottage, William said with a sparkle in his eyes, "That concludes our tour of the two shops in the town of Port Quin. It was my pleasure to escort you," he said, smiling. "I bid you good afternoon and a pleasant evening. Perhaps I could call on you again and soon." He stated rather than asked it, tipping his hat, and with a twinkle in his eye, turning and heading back through Quay Street. I watched as he turned left, up toward Kellan Head where he lived in a white house with his mother and apparently sometimes his father.

Standing at our front door, my mother said, "A gentle sort, that one. I like him. Run fetch a bucket and some water from the barn for dem lovely flowers, Effy dear."

"Yes, Mum." I turned and went around the side of the house, through the little gate and beside our kitchen garden to the back of the house to the small shed we referred to as our "barn." The day was so warm that I stopped in the cooler shade of the barn just for a moment, when I heard what sounded like a whimper or some small cries come from within. I stood still and heard it again—a muffled cry like that from a child. Was someone or something injured? I wanted to help. I crept over to the side of the barn as quietly as I could, so as not to frighten whatever was making the sound. I found a crack in the wood and I slowly looked through it with one eye. Inside were a few golden bundles of hay, our garden tools, scraps of wood for making chicken coops, the lobster pots, and the like.

I scanned the barn to determine what was making the sound. First, I looked downwards for an animal or small child. Then, as I looked to the back of the barn, I saw clothes lying in heaps on the floor. I started to panic as I saw, leaning forward on the hay, the rippled muscles of hairy, naked legs, a man's, and his naked white buttocks in the exact act that Parson Hockings was warning against less than a couple of hours before. I saw the pale white, thin open thighs of a woman. Her hair had come loose and fell in waves down to her waist. Her pale arms reached for the man and her hands looked tiny clutched to his muscular shoulders. On one of her slim wrists, I caught a glimpse of a shiny gold chain. A gift from him? I gasped, shrinking back, but clearly saw the black hair and side of my father's face with no mistake. I saw the large bulging naked breasts the tawny haired Cornelia, flopping and bouncing between her arms, as she sat, legs wide open, on a hay bale, her head and white neck tilted back. My father's hand was over her mouth, attempting to cover the sounds I had already heard, which were not those of someone in pain. She was not struggling or fighting. Clearly she was enjoying herself.

I grabbed up all my skirts to my knees quickly and quietly and I turned and ran. I prayed as I ran that I had not been detected. I could not fathom what my father would do to me if he knew what I had seen. I ran back to the house, my heart beating wildly, sweating, tears in my eyes. I wanted to vomit. My mind was racing about how to enter the house, how not to be found out, and how not to disgrace my mother. I must compose myself, I thought, and quickly caught my breath, opened the front door, blinking hard, and walked into the house. My most pleasant day had turned into an open wound.

Chapter Four

THE PASSIONS OF FLOWERS

PORT QUIN, CORNWALL, U.K.

AUGUST 2, 1841

I dropped the flowers on the kitchen table and went straight to the cupboard to find a tankard to put the flowers in. I blindly went to the basin to fill it with water. I stared down into the water unable to fully comprehend what I had just seen. My heart still pounding, I willed my breath to slow down.

"Did you find the bucket?" Mother asked cheerfully, her back to me while she washed dishes in the tub.

"I did," I lied. "But I thought the orchids would stand up much better in this tankard, so I am using this," I replied as cheerfully as I could. I grabbed the flowers off the table and stuffed them into the tankard and set them on the table, wiping my hands on my dress. Tears pricked my eyes again, but I blinked hard, pushing them back so that my mother wouldn't notice.

More than ever before, I hated my father with a passion. Hot feelings of pure loathing for his ugliness and disrespect of my mother filled my mind and body. My hatred was also mixed with fear as I realized that Cornelia was also my age, or younger. I had heard stories of drunken fathers molesting their own daughters. Would I be next? I had always feared that my father's or brother's crude talk and jokes about what they wanted to do to women would be used on me at some point. On some drunken evening or other. I had lived with this fear all my life.

I closed my eyes and remembered back to being a ten-year-old girl at this exact spot at the table. My father had come around the back of my mother's chair and gripped her chest from behind, crudely, and said, "I am imagining three times the size here!" He had laughed uproariously at his own joke. My mother simply brushed his hands away and carried on. To do that in front of his daughter had disgusted me and was very callus to Mother, I thought at the time and continued to think. How could he be so disrespectful to her? Why didn't either of us say anything to him? Because of the shame we felt and because we feared him, we said nothing and did nothing. He had a complete hold over us—we didn't dare say a word. We knew he could have us condemned in any manner of ways. If we wanted to continue living as we were used to, the only choice we had was to say nothing. Who would believe us over him? No one. We had no rights. No voice. No money of our own. Everything we had was his. Even I was his property in the eyes of the law.

Then there was the time when I was older, about twelve, when we stood on the quay at the end of the day. I accidentally dropped his favourite fishing net that he asked me to hold. I was carrying too many things at once. I dropped it lightly on the ground, standing in front of him and my friend Kensa. We had been playing on the beach and had run up the paths and alongside the harbour stopping beside his boat, the *Mary*. Happy to help, I gladly held the net, but I was tired, and it was a sweltering day, and the net slipped from my hand. The next thing I knew, Father punched me in the cheek with his fist. I fell back on the quayside, falling on my backside hard. None of the seamen milling about said a word. I remember running off to a hiding place after the incident, my cheek pounding in pain. I hid for hours with Kensa in a small cave along the cove. She and I never spoke about it. Father and I never spoke about it. *He has been a bully of our own making,* I thought. Now, when I opened my eyes, I was staring at the floor, gripping the back of the kitchen chair I stood behind, my teeth clenched.

My grandmother Elizabeth, my mother's mother, who came for supper every Sunday, eyed me from her woven chair in the corner. She sat so quietly, napping with her knitting in her lap, that I had forgotten she was there. Her white hair was coiled around the top of her head and her creased face looked like a pink shriveled apple. Second to Mother, Gran Elizabeth or "Gran" was my source of wisdom and kindness. "Effy, child. 'Av ye seed evil, child? What ails ye?" she croaked, pointing a crooked finger at me.

Thinking quickly and knowing how superstitious Gran was, I said, "When I was in the barn, it was dark, and I was frightened by an evil spirit or a ghost." I tried to relax. Gran thought and spoke about ghosts and the dark arts, which at times frightened me and my mother. Not wanting to get into that talk now, I picked up a stack of pewter plates and began setting them around the places at the table, carrying on as if everything was normal. "But it's no matter now." I smiled at her weakly and made a hexing sign to ward off evil as she had taught me. Her stare back at me told me she was not convinced.

Mother was preparing a rabbit stew with carrots and potatoes, but I had no appetite. Moments later, Father came in the back door and roughly said, "When's supper? Cade Bolitho's joinin'." He tossed his black suit jacket and hat down on the bench next to the back door and rubbed his face and nose with his white shirt sleeve. The underarms and front of his shirt were streaked with sweat. Mother and I would have to work hard to get his shirt white again, but that was not something he cared about.

"Effy, set another place at the table," Mother calmly said while I stood stock still, frozen in place, as my father walked around the kitchen, stuffing a few cut carrots in his mouth, and thankfully taking no notice of me. "Go on now," Mother chided.

I went to the cupboard and pulled out another pewter plate and utensils. I found it odd that Father invited Cade to supper. I could feel my own heartbeat in my ears, as my heart was pounding so hard. He hadn't been invited before. *Why didn't Father ask me first about this? Another sign that I mean nothing.* But that was Father. Father was friendly with the Bolitho family and encouraged Cade where I was concerned.

As the afternoon drew on towards evening it was hot and humid. The atmosphere in the house was tense, like walking on hot stones with bare feet. I looked at Mother to see if she seemed to notice anything wrong, but if she did, she did not let on. I continued to help Mother in the kitchen, stirring the stew from time to time, looking down into the simmering pot to avoid conversation with anyone. I dreaded having Cade come to supper, imagining what he would say about William walking me home from church.

"What went on 'ere today?" Father asked in his deep terse voice.

"The usual net mindin' and knittin'," Mother replied, as she checked on the softness of the boiled potatoes.

"You need to pull more weight round here, Mary. I can't work no faster. We need cash for the things we need, ye know." He threw himself down on a chair, clearly exhausted, his face and neck grimy.

"I 'ave sold several pints of honey ale and extra servings of rabbit stew to Mr. Kellow for the inn," Mother replied, wiping her hand on a towel. She looked at him with a deliberately blank expression. "More of those parties has come for a month-long stay at Doyden castle, and Mr. Kellow needs meals quick. He come here yesterday morn and asked for anything I could provide and said he would pay cash."

"Mother, what a clever idea. You know how Mr. Kellow fancies your rabbit stew," I offered, hoping to encourage Mother's opportunity to raise money for the family. Melly, my dear friend, and her father, Mr. Kellow, had been our guests for supper many times over the years. "Of course, I'll be happy to help you."

"Bah! Hold your noise, woman. Stew!" Father sneered. "A pittance," he muttered, shaking his head. "And you! Miss high an' mighty with the surgery! What bloody consarn be that of yourn?" Father often broke out into a stream of cursing when he was like this, yelling about men's genitalia and profane acts which made my skin crawl and want to hide under a bed or behind a door, which I often did as a child. Nothing any woman would ever want to hear.

Mother broke in quickly before he could go on any more about the surgery. "I also have wool to dye to make several shawls to sell in Isaac as the weather gits cooler," she added, her hands on her hips and looking him in the eyes now. "My shawls brought in good coin last year." She had more to say to him, but he lumbered off towards the bedroom, apparently to get cleaned up for supper.

"Oh, that old yarn!" He grumbled, paused, and then laughed at his own joke; his bulky shoulders bouncing up and down with glee.

I raised my eyebrows at Mother. She said nothing. I gave her a look of thanks for keeping him off the subject of my work at the surgery. She turned to continue her preparations for the meal at hand.

Only moments later, Cade came to the door, as boisterous as ever. Father strode over, suddenly full of energy, and let him in. Father and Cade slapped each other on the back in greeting. I watched them and it seemed to me Father was more than happy to have another male in the house. Father liked Cade because he was a strong, manly type and a good fisherman who didn't back down from any storm or any fight.

"Anything doin' last week, Cade me boy?" Father asked, letting Cade in the door as Cade took off his hat.

"Nothin' doin'. Very few caught yesterday. You?" Cade asked, shrugging his large shoulders.

"Thin. Very thin," Father replied, turning to take a seat.

Father and Cade sat down in the front room, and Father asked Cade about the schooner *Brilliant* from Penzance harbour that had recently wrecked in a storm and what became of the crew.

"Drowned, all of 'em, even the captain," Father explained, with a dramatic wave of his hand.

"God protect us. Was that sartin?" Cade asked.

"Ain't got one alive," Father responded.

Father sat with his long legs spread wide open and his elbows on his knees. His big hands dangled down except when they were needed to add to the story. "The entire load of slate lost, I were told. Despite a recue bid from Newquay's schooner *Sisters,* all the crew were lost," Father continued.

"Tragic, that. What was the tonnage, do you reckon?" Cade asked with interest, intent on the story.

"Dunno," Father replied. "Did ye hear about the *Mary Stuart* of Cardiff off Praa Sands in Mounts Bay? Now that were a blowing gale!"

I turned from their conversation to slicing hot bread for the stew and placing it in a basket for the table. "Supper is served," Mother announced, and Cade and Father came to the table and sat down.

Father slapped his hands together and said, "I could eat twelve Mackerel in one sitting and drink the water they were boiled in!" Gran, Mother, and I joined, pulling our chairs in.

Cade smiled at me and said, "Effy, lovely to see you again after church today."

"And you, Cade." I smiled back, unsure of what to say.

"The stew smells wonderful," Cade said, smiling again at

Mother and me. "How do you make the stew smell so enticing? What do you put in it?"

"You probably smell the sage and onions. That along with the browned rabbit creates a savory smell. It is delicious, isn't it?" I added. I tried to make light conversation, but I was still stinging from the sight of my father in the barn and now from the appearance of Cade at my dinner table. What was Cade on about tonight? Certainly, he was here for more than seafaring tales of shipwrecks with Father. My suspicion was that he would try to wedge himself in between William and me. I was on tenterhooks.

Mother smiled in return and then pressed her hands together and bent her head down to say the blessing and we all did likewise. She prayed, "Father, for what we are receivin', may we be truly grateful. Amen."

"Amen," my father said, just before stuffing a spoon full of stew in his mouth.

"Amen," we all said in unison. We began to eat, our utensils clinking against our plates.

"Lovely flowers, Mrs. Pengelly. Did you pick 'em yourself?" Cade asked Mother, in an innocent tone. Surely he knew exactly who had picked those flowers, I thought, confused.

Mother paused. "No, I didn't," she said, dipping her spoon back to her plate. She politely smiled at Cade but said nothing more.

"Then you, Effy. You pick 'em?" Caden asked, a slight edge in his voice this time.

I was stunned. I saw immediately where he was going with his question. I considered my options. Either I bent the truth and said I picked the flowers, or I avoided the question. "No,

Cade. I didn't," I said, focusing on my stew and trying to drop the subject.

Sternly this time, Cade asked, "I see. Then who did pick these flowers?"

Everyone sat still at the table. I swallowed and tried to speak. Father leaned his elbows on the table and loudly said, "Effy, Cade asked you a question. Who picked dem flowers?"

When my father spoke like that, I became anxious and nervous because of his emotional and physical violence towards me in the past. I remembered times when my father had kicked me repeatedly over something one of my brothers had done. The shame and humiliation bubbled up in me. "William Carlyon, Father. He picked the flowers," I said, meeting Father's eyes directly, trying not to seem apologetic. *I am a grown woman. I have done nothing inappropriate or wrong.*

"That pirate's son? That feckin' criminal? What the 'ell, Effy?" Father said, his eyes bearing down on me, his large upper body looming over the table. *This was no show for Cade*, I thought to myself. *He truly despises William and his family for being outsiders, for having more wealth than us.*

"I..." I stammered, shaking my head, embarrassed, confused, and afraid of what my father might say in front of Cade. I looked around the table at Mother and Gran, who sat silently with resigned expressions on their faces.

"No dattur of mine be mixing with his lot. That'll be the end of dat, for sure." Father declared, almost happily, nudging Cade with his elbow. "Now, where d'em pilchards be running next Cade, me boy?"

Cade looked down at his plate and smiled.

Chapter Five

Dripping Hopes and Dreams

Port Quin, Cornwall, U.K.

August 3, 1841

The next morning, I was in a foul mood. But Father seemed quite happy, standing at the door with his lunch and cap, ready to leave for the quay, probably because of his victory with Cade last night at supper. But I was still angry about his interference with William.

"Goin' out with only four pots, Effy? Your brothers carry six!" he sneered as I passed him on my way from the barn carrying the smelly pots. I said nothing in return, but I wanted to lash out, "Huzah for them!" I wanted to scream at him, "Don't you see me trying to do my best?" But I knew my place. Keep quiet. Absorb his harsh words and say nothing. Don't react—that's what he wants you to do so that he can beat you back. Endure it today, like every day. Scorn was all I or my mother could hope to achieve from him. That's how it was. A bitter taste we always swallowed. I held my breath as I passed. Thankfully, he said no more.

The last thing I wanted to do today, tired and aching as I was from yesterday's work, was to set up the withy pots to catch lobsters—my least favorite chore, which Father certainly knew. To do so meant crawling out amongst the slippery rocks in my long skirts, most certainly getting soaking wet, and having to walk back hours later soaked again and with heavy pots filled with lobsters. If they were not full of the angry, scuttling, clawed beasts, more would be the trouble I'd be in.

Luckily, I would have Melwynn for company today, as I had convinced her to join me in the pot setting to get lobsters for the Turbot Inn. She would take her catch directly to her father and I would haul mine up the road toward Roscarwyn farm to sell them to Mr. Adams who would then put them on his fish cart going to Port Isaac. He would in turn then sell them and any other fish he had to Mrs. Barrett. She was a heavy woman who had lost both arms in an accident. She ran a small grocery shop in Port Isaac. Above her shop was a small room which she let to tenants; she also kept a gaggle of noisy children in a sort of school room below. I had heard that she kept the children entertained by singing little toons but often those toons came in the order of shouts of, "Sit down you stinkin' elephants!" swinging a stout cane she held under her armpit when she needed them to sit on the little bench in her school room.

The quay was springing to life this as every morning as the seaman boarded their vessels like ants on an anthill—busily working each task to make ready for the sea. Most of the working boats were luggers with their flat-bottomed hulls, shallow draught, and the rig, which made them highly maneuverable in the shallow Port Quin waters and enabled sailing against the strong and ever-present winds. I greeted old Mr. Lacombe, my next-door neighbor, as he puffed his pipe that dangled from his clenched teeth.

"Watch out for rabbits, Mr. Lacombe!" I laughed, as he and his crew pushed off the *Rochester* from its mooring. I knew Mr. Lacombe was very superstitious about rabbits causing empty nets.

"Never mention bleddy rabbits. That's the worst of the lot. Never mention they!" He shouted at me over his shoulder. I laughed to myself.

"G'Day, Effy." Mr. Hicks waved from the bow of the *Rochester* with a slight smile. Seamen didn't seem to smile much these days given their catches had been mostly thin of late.

"How's the wind today, Mr. Hicks?" I called after him, He was known to be able to whistle up the wind, which my father hated and claimed was never true.

"Fair to middlin. Might have to whistle it up!" He cried out. And with that, the *Rochester,* the *Mary,* and all the other fishing boats were either off to sea or about ready to be cast off.

I met up with Melly at the quay and she waved at me as I approached. She was a sight for sore eyes! Melly was always ready with her crooked smile and pleasant disposition. She had a plain face with several round small pegs of skin that had grown near her eyes and on her chin. With her stout look of a Cornish woman, her thick calves could climb any cliff path with ease. I often wondered how she remained so pleasant and then I reminded myself that her father was as equally as pleasant as she was. My mood changed just by being near her.

We both wore our heavy, round-toed black boots to protect our feet and shins against the mussels that clung to the rocks, their shiny black shells glistened in the sun between tides. Our straw bonnets did their best to protect our eyes from the stinging glare of the sun on the water. I rolled my shirt sleeves up to keep them as clean as I could. No use getting them dirty only to have to scrub them later.

I regaled her with my torment from the night before as we carefully tramped along the shore of the bay. The boats were now well out to sea, and we talked as we began to set our pots for the unsuspecting lobsters lurking in the rock pools.

"So, ye think Cade done thought dat, 'bout the flowers, all along, do ye?" Melly asked. "He's a schemer, that one."

"Yes, I do. And I think he planned to get Father involved too." I said as I waded into the water. Surf splashed up on my legs as I tried to get my pot as close as I could to the larger rocks. As I tried to avoid cutting my fingers yet again on the sharp edges of the mix of mussel and barnacle shells, I lowered my first baited pot down in what I thought was a good place for luring lobsters. My skirts were getting wet, and I was having difficulty holding the pot. I hated having to walk in wet skirts. The feeling of wet clothing clinging to my legs and boots annoyed me and made it difficult to walk.

"Oh, bleddy hell, Melly." Out of sheer frustration, I dropped the pot on a nearby rock and lifted all my skirts over my thighs. I looped the back of them through the front, tying them in a knot.

"Effy!" Melly cried out. "Your legs is bare! You mustn't! You'll git the strap for that!"

"No one is in sight," I said, looking out to sea and waving

my arm at its vastness. My legs might be bare, but my skirts will be dry by the end of this!" I set all three of my pots in the water and stumbled back to the sandy beach. I found a large flat dry rock and lay on my back, the droplets on my legs glistening in the sun. I closed my eyes. Melly continued splashing about with her pots.

"Melly, if I wasn't here setting up these dirty, smelly pots trying not to get cut by mussels, I could be doing something really important with my life," I sighed.

"Like what? We've got to 'ave food, an all," Melly insisted.

"I know. I know. But I think I could be doing more to help with sicknesses," I said, sitting up right with my hands behind me.

"Here's some seaweed for your tonics," she said, throwing a handful of brownish green, slimy seaweed on my legs, laughing.

"An excellent side dish for the Turbot Inn!" I said with a smile.

After a while I thought about telling Melly about the premonition at the church but decided against it as Melly was easily frightened about the black arts. Instead, I decided to ask her about William and his family. "Melly, do you think William— William Carlyon that is—is from a pirate family? Really?"

"Not sure since they ain't from here. Never seed 'em afore. They seem like dey is sometimes," she said. "A bit mysterious, like."

"Yes, but not malicious," I replied in concentration. "William wants to be a boatbuilder. Isn't that admirable, Melly? He can use his mind and his hands. And he speaks so well! He is educated. To hear him talk about it...I don't know. His mind is so set on it. Like he can make anything happen. I wish I could say the same for myself," I sighed.

"Yes. I wish I done got a lobster or two here and now." She smiled and took my hand because she knew the keenness of my frustration.

"There's no way out of Port Quin, is there Melly? No way beyond these pots and nets for us, I mean." I asked, looking around me at the rocks. Sea gulls circled over us hoping for a meal. "The men are free to take on many jobs. They can work on the boats, in the mills, on the farms, and they can own property, and move to another town or village on their own if they like. Roam about unaccompanied. They are free. Even go to school if they like and have the means. Even build ships. But what are we, Melly? We are just pairs of hands without minds. We don't think, we just do." I pulled my skirts down, resuming my more respectable appearance. My dour mood was returning.

"Dunno. Somebody got to do the work an' the men done it too. We girls could work on a farm and all. C'mon. It ain't so bad. Pa got dem saffron buns. Let's get dem and come back later and see if we got lobsters." She smiled her crooked smile that I loved so much, and I couldn't resist her. We walked back to the Turbot Inn as clouds gathered overhead, adding to my gloom. My skirts were dry but in my mind my hopes and dreams were dampened. Nevertheless, the wheels in my head kept turning over the one real way forward that I saw for myself.

Chapter Six

SLIDING SHINY RIVULETS

PORT QUIN, CORNWALL, U.K.

AUGUST 6, 1841

Days later, I still stung with hurt and embarrassment from Cade's control and trickery of my father at the supper table and my father's sordid actions with Cornelia. Cade and my father were obviously of one mind and a strong force that left me feeling dejected and powerless in comparison. The remainder of that evening had gone no better.

I went to the surgery early and put on a clean white apron over my neck. The surgery smelled scrubbed and crisp with a hint of mint and lavender. The smell instantly comforted me and reminded me of possibilities outside my troubled home life. As I looked through the thick glass of the window at the light, drizzly rain, downcast, as hot tears pricked my eyes. My mother and grandmother had done nothing to help me at the supper table that night and said nothing afterwards. Were we women so afraid of our men as to not utter a single word? If so, then we were in fact powerless, completely subservient in a man's world. I felt all my hope and energy draining out of me.

I was watching out the window for Dr. Moyle's arrival. The rain drops slid down the windowpane, slowly at first. Trickling down unhurriedly, then gaining speed, and falling helplessly to form rivulets that spread in different directions downward. Some drops dared to form colours of the rainbow when slivers of light hit them, and others were shiny silver. Several of the rivulets formed together and as they became heavier, formed tiny streams hurling down to face whatever fate lay below as a larger body of water. *If only we women banded together like that*, I thought, my mood dampened. Still, at the surgery I could be myself, which gave me strength to face the day. There I felt safe. Hopeful.

I was glad to escape my spinning, washing, weeding and those lobster pots to assist Dr. Moyle. He was a pleasant, intelligent, and calm thirty-five-year-old man of stout build with a thick, black beard who lived with his wife and four children near Kellan Head. He was frequently called to help the surgeon in Port Isaac in addition to his duties in Port Quin. He traveled on his horse the two miles between the ports on the undulating grassy path between the hedges carrying his medical bag and equipment. Dr. Moyle was an educated man, a trained surgeon, and a gentleman. Not of the lower order like me, my family, and friends. I had been studying not only his medical practices, but his personal grooming and manner of speech for years, as I still did today, as I wondered what life was like for him and his wife. He spoke very clearly, pronouncing the sound of every letter, of course. That is how one could tell right away that he was from the upper class. That and his manner of dress. He was always dressed very properly, with a cravat, like he was going to church, even during the week. And his posture was different from ours. He stood tall and erect, and never slouched like the men of the lower class often did. His mannerisms were always delicate and polite. He never spit on the ground or wiped his nose on his sleeve. Even his teeth were different, as white as beached seashells rather than yellow or even black as many of our neighbors' teeth were.

I studied him because I wanted to be like him. I wanted to be an educated, well mannered, clear speaking, clean and erect woman of means. Perhaps women in the upper classes were treated differently, better, than women in the lower classes. Not beaten physically and mentally. Not made to do the most menial of jobs for hours on end and then made to take care of the animals and the men too. I imagined their bodies and hands didn't ache from overwork every day. Maybe they even had their own money to spend. I could read, taught by my mother, and was determined to use Dr. Moyle to better myself. Even if I wasn't in the upper classes and likely never would be, striving to be there and making progress by inches was better to me than doing nothing and living hopelessly in vulgarity, as I had heard some of the upper class in St. Isaac call us.

I often tried to imagine what it would be like to be an upper-class woman. An educated woman of means. I didn't know any upper-class women, but in my mind they were carefree and spent their day reading books. Many books about places they would take their children. Fantastic cities where they would sit in parks and attend plays and church. Women in the upper-class had no worries or chores to do, in my mind. They spent their days in a kind of delicious solitude during both the day and as a kind of blue evening fell, reading and sitting in their gardens with their husbands, perhaps. Was this the sort of life I wanted? I wasn't sure but I wanted to learn more and to read more than our single book, the Bible.

When he arrived, I reminded myself of how hard I would have to fight for any education, since Dr. Moyle was my only foreseeable path forward.

"You all right, then?" Dr. Moyle asked, the standard town greeting, shaking off the rain as he came into our humble surgery, and I shook myself out of my daydreams. "Effy, you are a Godsend to have here. I see you have clean bandages at the ready for placing into the cupboards. Have you crushed the mint and the willow bark for the tonics?" Dr. Moyle was all work when he came, as was typical, as his visits to Port Quin were short, and he usually had an abundance of patients.

"Yes, Dr. Moyle, I have. You have eight patients to visit today, all homebound with respiratory ailments. I took the liberty of making the possets and the mint teas for them, packed here and ready for you," I said, proudly pointing to the packages wrapped in cloths and tied with twine. "I also added a package of seaweed so that you can treat Mrs. Hambley's rheumatism."

"Excellent. Well done, Effy. If you can, make more of those mint teas. More people will undoubtedly come down with the same ailment, and that will put us in good stead for Thursday when the surgery is open next. Can you manage that and handle anyone that comes in? You're well able to attend to the usual burns, cuts, bruises, and the like. And make sure they pay, will you? Hardly anyone who comes in pays," he said, muttering under his breath. "When I return, I intend to start your training on mending broken bones. Would that suit you?"

"Yes, I'm happy to learn anything you feel I can take on, Dr. Moyle," I replied.

"Tell anyone that requires me that I'm out but will be back in the middle of the afternoon, will you?"

"Of course, Dr. Moyle. I will. Is there anything else you require?"

"Yes, will you please refill my bottle with pure rainwater from the back? While it's wet out now, it is so blasted hot when the sun comes out! At least all the summer storms we've had gave us fresh water a plenty," Dr. Moyle sighed, rubbing his face.

"Right away, Dr. Moyle," I said, quickly taking his bottle and rushing out the back door to the rainwater cistern. I gently dipped the bottle into the cool water which felt so clear and clean I wanted to plunge my entire body in it.

Dr. Moyle was stuffing the last of his needed supplies into his pack when I handed him the bottle. He looked at me and started to speak, then closed his mouth as if he decided against it.

"Something wrong, Dr. Moyle?" I asked.

"Oh, it's just that thieves have been robbing newly dug graves again, causing trouble in the village. A lot of speculation, you know, about who is doing it. People are troubled about disturbing the dead, you know. Whole bodies or body parts are missing. A nasty business, and all supposedly in the cause of science! You don't know anything about this, do you?"

He sheepishly eyed me, as if regretting having asked me almost at once.

"No, Dr. Moyle. I don't know anything about that," I responded, looking at him and wondering why someone would do such a terrible thing.

"Of course not," he answered, waving his hand, and muttering to himself again. "Well, I'm off, then. Make sure you ask for payment, Effy. How do people expect me to operate a surgery without payments?" He grumbled, let out and angry sigh of frustration, and then quickly said, "I bid you good day." Stopping suddenly at the door, he gave me a long, curious smile, almost a glare. He then pulled open the door and left. I had never seen him in quite such a peculiar mood.

No sooner had Dr. Moyle gone than William rode up in his horse drawn wagon. I wasn't expecting to see him, but it was as if the sun pulled out of the clouds and shone brilliantly the instant he came into view through the open doorway. William and his family owned the only wagon in town, and it was much sought after for any number of problems. He always shared the wagon with anyone in need, which puzzled me. Why would a family of pirates, if they were such a thing, be so willing to share their prized wagon to help others? Another reason in my mind that the Carlyons were not pirates at all, but I wouldn't be discussing this with Father.

"Good day to you, William. What brings you here? Not ill, I hope?" I said, standing in the doorway as he jumped lithely down from the wagon. He circled to the back and fumbled through some straw with his gloved hands.

"Halloo, Effy. You're looking bright today. No, not ill, thank ye. I came with a patient, though." Through the straw he pulled out a newborn lamb, white as snow, and held it in the crook of his arm. The pink nosed lamb let out a very weak *baaahhh* at the sight of me. It was love at first sight for both of us.

"Oh, heavenly days! Who is this precious babe? Very late in the season for a new lamb, isn't it?" I asked, stroking the lamb's chin, and then looking up at William with questioning and excited eyes.

"It certainly is. I found him lying on the side of the road. Separated from his mother, I take it. He looks weak and sickly. I thought you might be able to nurse him," he said, with a nod of his head towards the surgery door.

"Yes, of course, but let's bring him around the back where I have water. I'll find a glove and a knife."

We went through the surgery picking up the things that I needed. I quickly cut a sliver in a thin glove and filled it with water mixed with a small amount of willow bark to relieve pain. William held the lamb in his lap as we sat on a gray stone bench, the mist swirling around us like a cloak. He seemed to be studying me as he held the lamb, and I held the glove as the lamb greedily sucked.

"He's guzzling it down, the poor thing!" I exclaimed. "You did well to bring him here as I fear he may not have survived otherwise. He should have milk, which I can get at home for him," I said, calmly stroking the lamb's flanks as he sucked from the glove.

"He can be a strong little fellow. A bit of care and he will make it just fine." William smiled. "I knew you would know what to do."

I smiled in return, our hands and arms brushing as the

lamb shifted and struggled to keep close to the glove. We laughed and enjoyed the moment in the misty rain.

"A name," I said. "What shall we name this charming boy?" I scratched the lamb's chest and gave a sigh of relief.

"I don't know. Let me see. He is hungry. Maybe about hunger. Or something about being strong. Like granite. Or boulders," William offered.

I laughed, "Yes, something strong but maybe with a touch more of a living element, like Moses. Moses, from the Bible, was very strong."

"Moses. It suits him well," William replied, stroking the lamb with his large, strong looking hands. A pause followed. His eyes found mine, and I suddenly felt nervous.

"Effy, in truth I also came by to tell you something." William took my free hand in his and his eyes locked mine. I felt so wonderfully warm and accepted at that moment. I simply looked up and waited for him to go on.

"I hope you see the truth in my words. You are the most beautiful person I have ever met, inside and out." I looked at him in surprise, my eyes widening. He continued, "I can see the kindness in your heart. The way you care for those around you. It fills me with hope. Sometimes I feel trapped here in Port Quin. But one person, other than my family, keeps me here." He looked at me with that same magnetic look in his eyes. "You know what people say of my family, that we're pirates and robbers. None of that is true. My father is often away seeking capital for our boat building business. I would like to have more time with you, and I hope that you might consider walking out with me. That is, I am asking you if you might consider courting me."

I could feel my face softening and a broad smile took over my face. I looked at him with a newfound appreciation that a man might finally see me for who I truly was and find value in that.

"I have been hoping you would see me in that way," I whispered, my voice carrying over the sound of the rain.

"I absolutely do. Give me the chance to show you what if means to be with someone who treasures the beauty and knowledge within you." His deep voice had become choked with a passion that was barely contained.

"I too see your goodness. I feel it. I would be proud to be with you, William," I said, my eyes never leaving his.

"I see other men, like Cade, who also desire you, but that desire comes from a hunger to have you as a conquest. Do you understand what that means?" William asked.

"I understand completely. But Cade is harmless. We have been loving friends since childhood. That is all," I tried to assure William but was uneasy inside about Cade myself.

"Well then, I am pleased beyond measure. My mother and I would like to invite you over for supper any time you are free. And in the meantime, can I help you home with Moses or would you like me to take him to my home? I have a stall I could use for him..." William trailed off thinking out loud.

"A stall for what? Isn't this a cozy scene. Hallo, William. Hallo Effy, love," Cade said as he appeared from nowhere on foot from the lane behind the surgery. William and I looked at each other, startled by Cade's sudden appearance. I for one wondered what he might have overheard and how long he might have been hovering nearby, listening to our conversation.

I quickly recovered from being startled. "William has found a sickly lamb and I have agreed to care for it. I call him Moses." I said, standing up and pulling Moses into my arms, his little mouth dripping.

"I see. Yes, he does seem a bit young to be out on the town without his mother," Cade laughed.

"I will need to nurse him every hour or so until he is stronger, so I should take him home," I decided.

"Of course, Effy. I could build a pen for Moses, if you like, out beside your barn. I am sure your father would approve of that, until the lamb is stronger and can be returned to its rightful owner," Cade said, a bit unfeelingly. I clutched Moses to my chest at the idea of returning him somewhere, perhaps prematurely. "Haven't seen you around the Turbot lately, Will," Cade continued.

"Too busy," William replied. "Besides, inn life makes you soft." The two appeared to be sparring about something and I wondered if I was the cause of their terse tones. "How have the parties been at the Castle, Cade?" William asked, standing to his full height, his hands on his hips.

"Dunno. T'es not my affair. I haven't been to any 'parties' at Doyden Castle if there are any. I have been there to drop things off for Mr. Symons, the owner. That's about it," Cade replied.

"What parties at the Doyden Castle?" I asked. I often wondered what happened up on the hill to the south of Port Quin in the mysterious and oddly small castle.

"Never you mind," Cade responded. William raised his eyebrows as if he knew more than he was letting on.

"I would like that pen for Moses, Cade," I said as we

watched Cade stride inside the back door and take off his coat as if he planned to stay.

"Might you have some tea about, Effy? I would like a tankard full if you have it as I am mighty thirsty." Cade looked at William with a low glance, his hands flexing at his sides. His glance was like a silent, low guttural snarl.

William was ready to leave. I went outside with him and pulled the door closed behind me. "Please come by this evening and check on Moses if you can. I will be home after supper, and we could walk around the headland."

"That sounds perfect. I'll come by then," he said, and he gave me a wink. He had carried along a length of rope with Moses. He tied an intricate loop and knot and slipped it lightly over Moses' head and tied the loose end to the leg of the stone bench. He gave the lamb a comforting scratch behind one ear and then agilely stood and turned the corner to return to his horse and wagon.

I opened the door and went inside to make Cade his tea as I heard William's wagon wheels rolling down the lane towards the village. I found Cade seated at the consulting table, looking down at his fingernails, which seemed unusually clean to me, smiling. I was surprised that no one had come to the surgery so far that morning. The day had been unusually quiet. I made the tea sparingly, as tea was expensive and Dr. Moyle only had tea for medicinal purposes and set the steaming cup in front of him.

"Ah, just what I need!" He sighed, breathing in a whiff of the tea's aroma. "I hope it's strong," he quipped, taking a quick sip. "I haven't slept in days."

"Sadly, it is not," I replied. "Dr. Moyle only allows weak

teas here," I added. "Why no sleep?"

"Never you mind. Not to worry. You look well today, love. How are you?" Cade asked, taking me in as if I was a full painting to be admired.

"I am quite well, thank you. But I am very cross with you, Cade, over your performance at supper the other evening. I don't like how you and Father are in league together. I expect to be busy today, Cade, so I don't have time for visitors," I said.

"Oh, you will have time to hear what I have come to say," Cade murmured.

"And what that might be?" I asked, very annoyed, turning to put the tea caddy back in the cupboard.

"Effy, I have come to tell you," he said, pushing his cup aside and taking my hands in his. He pulled me into a chair facing him. "I have come to tell you that I have asked your father a very important question regarding the two of us and he has said yes to that question. So, I ask that you meet me at the front steps of the church this evening."

I was stunned. I had always been drawn to Cade, the way he carried himself with such confidence and strength. He had that inner grit that I admired. I felt a painful tug at my heartstrings, a feeling I had never experienced before. A mix of flattery and confusion. I was tongue tied.

"Cade. What can you mean by this?" I asked in a panic.

He looked at me, like he was happy that I was surprised.

"Yes, it is sudden and a surprise but also a happy one. Because that is how we will be, " he responded.

"I will need some time to think..," I stammered. "And I cannot possibly come tonight. I have plans already."

"Plans? What kind of plans? Change them, of course!"

Cade was adamant.

"No, I can't. That is, Mother. I have plans with Mother and I also have Moses to care for tonight." I explained. His eyes beckoned me, and his hands crept up my arms, pulling me closer.

"And you are in league with my father and he is too hard on Mother and me, Cade," I warned.

"I am nothing like him but I do want his blessing where you are concerned. You know I would never hurt or miss treat you. Have I ever hurt you?" He asked his eyes roving mine. I had to admit he never had. "Then tomorrow night and no excuses. Think about what you will wear and say to me tomorrow night on the church steps as we begin our romance, finally, in earnest. I have waited so long for you," Cade said. He pulled me towards him, and his face was inches from mine. His face up close was even handsome than from farther away.

"Cade, this is not a good idea and definitely not fitting," I said, pushing him away but all the while I felt a hot streak flash and sharp tingling between my legs. He placed his forehead on mine and his arms encircled my waist in a heated embrace that pulled me into his lap. My lips craved to touch his so much that I thought any instant that I would succumb completely. I could feel his breath and his longing for me was dizzying, intoxicating. He nuzzled my face with his in a way that was so wanton I felt limp. I ached for him and couldn't pull away.

"No one has to know what we do..." he whispered in my ear as his tongue swept across my neck. I let out an uncontrollable sigh. My heart pounded.

"Halloo. Is anyone here? I have come to see Dr. Moyle..." a nasally female voice meekly said at the front door.

"Blast. I should have locked that bleddy door!" Cade cursed as I sprung from his lap to the front door.

I was throbbing with a sense of longing throughout my body and confusion coursed through my mind because it was William I wanted.

Chapter Seven

From Inside the Grave

Port Quin, Cornwall, U.K.

August 6, 1841

I pulled the hood of my blue light woollen cape over my calico bonnet and up closer around my face as the rain had grown heavier during the day. The wind whipped at the trees and leaves darted this way and that before me as I closed and locked the surgery door. I was eager to get home to see how Moses was doing and to give him another feeding. I packed his nursing glove in my satchel and headed down the path towards the church on my way home. I knew Mother would react kindly to our new family member, and I prayed that Father would allow Moses to stay.

Even though it was summer, and the afternoon sky should have shown plenty of light, the heavens were a light charcoal colour, and I was fearful. The bark on the trees was black, wet with rain, giving the path a spiky trim. Green leaves were turned light side up in warning of more rain. Walking alone in dim light was never a good idea, even during the daytime. Hungry and poor men and women, even children, could do foul things to a young woman walking alone, my mother always warned. Best never to be out alone. Ever. After the safety of the surgery, I felt exposed and I had a three mile walk ahead of me. And the wind and the rain chilled my skin in addition to goose bumps in my mind, so I began to hurry along the muddy path.

I ruminated about my unusual day as I walked on the uneven path, dodging puddles. The early afternoon had turned out to be busy after I managed to get Cade out the door. How was I to think about his question and our meeting tomorrow? The mud sucked at my boots on the path as my mind turned our conversation over and over. On the one hand, Cade was considered a "good catch" among the single women near and far. And he stirred a fire in me. On the other hand, I didn't want to fall into the same tragic trap my mother had with her marriage. No, I wanted to avoid that no matter what. And what about William? Wasn't he an even better catch? Yes, William had the intelligence and the grit I desired and was the answer to a better future, I decided. *Would I dare go against my father and walk out with William tonight? Of course, I would.* William was the one I wanted. I knew it in my heart and down to my bones. I couldn't wait to see him again even though I had just spoken to him only hours before.

The decrepit St. Minver's came into view amongst the trees off to the left of the path. Even though I was happy thinking about Moses and William and our walk on the Head, I noticed that strange feeling of dread come over me again, like the one I had felt in the church after the christening and sermon. A feeling of loss that was unexplainable. I slowed my steps for a moment.

Through the rain, I saw the tilted, grey headstones against the green of the trees in the background. I had the sense that I could feel thoughts coming from the headstones. Feelings of loss. Of mourning. Very powerful feelings of loved ones lost, never to return. *Of course, this is natural to feel at a graveyard,* I told myself, as I gawped at the graves. I forced myself to continue walking.

As I got closer, I began to hear the low pitiful moaning again. I distinctly heard wails of fear and anguish coming from inside the graves, but I knew this time the sounds I heard were not human. I had never heard anything like this before. The sounds were ghoulish and other worldly. I stopped because I could not believe what I was hearing, and I looked around frantically. No one was about.

The wind whipped down my hood and tore at my bonnet. My skirts flew about my shins and the strength of the wind blurred my eyes, making it difficult to see clearly. The church and graveyard stood between me and home, so I had to push on and get beyond it, but the howling sounds terrified me. I tried to run forward but couldn't. My heart was pounding in an ugly way.

An unknown force seemed to tilt my head down until I saw what was at my feet. Graves. Side by side on the edge of the path and not far from the front door of the church. Four graves lay open, the first two being the likes of which Dr. Moyle had mentioned earlier that day—robbed of their occupants and collecting rainwater. The wind seemed to keep my head looking down into the wet, muddy graves. I tried to resist looking but felt compelled by this strange and powerful force to do so. The sense of dread I felt grew stronger and stronger and became the sickening feeling of being with someone at the hour of their death, helpless to do anything. The smell of rotting flesh was so repugnant, I gagged. I covered my nose with my cape.

Then came something even worse, something I couldn't fathom even as I was seeing it with my own eyes. My heart convulsed in pain when I was forced to look into the third grave, now half filled with muddy water: There lay Cade's body, dressed in his Sunday best. His face was almost purple and pointed up, looking up at me with his eyes open and moving. He was trying to say something, but I pulled back from the fearsome sight with all my bodily strength. Terror pulled away any sound I tried to make. How was this possible? I tried to close my eyes, but they sprang open to see the contents of the fourth grave, which lay just two feet from the third. My own father, his black hair soaked, dressed in his seafaring gear, stared at me from inside the grave. I shrieked as his long arms sprang towards me in an instant. I fell backwards, sprawling, into the chunks of earth that had come from the empty graves. My father sat up and turned to say something to me, his face contorted in horror. The next thing I knew, I was clutching on to a tree off the path but safely past the church.

All was quiet. I was panting and gasping for air. The rain continued and the wind whirled and twisted branches all around me. Birds darted for safety. I blinked my eyes and slowly turned around to see what might be behind me back in the direction of the church. Only the churchyard, surrounding trees, and rocks lay silent behind me. The church sat crouched in its same, crumbling position that it had for hundreds of years. The tall spire with the cross on it still towered over the humble scene. The lichen covered gravestones were all still and held their usual positions.

My fingers and nails clung to the tree bark as if the strength of the tree would save me from the terrible thing I had just seen. Frightened tears rolled down my cheeks. *What had I just seen?* I concluded that I must have had a premonition come over me like I the one inside the church, only stronger. Never, ever had I had a premonition like this. But what did it *mean?* Something. *What was coming over me? Was I becoming some type of evil being? Was evil trying to take me over?* I felt like I was becoming some kind of monster. I tried to soothe myself. I tried to straighten my skirts in the wind. I must have been overcome with a dream, or maybe I ate something strange from the garden. A rare weed that causes strange dreams, perhaps. But I didn't recall anything unusual in anything I had eaten. I wiped my face with my sleeve and took a restorative breath. I had experienced a nightmare during the day, perhaps. I would discuss this with Grandmother, for sure. But no one else. I would hide this terrible thing where no one could ever know.

Feeling weakened but my powers of reason mostly regained, I released the tree, found my dropped satchel on the path, and struggled towards home. I knew I would never forget whatever it was I had just experienced. I realized that something lay ahead of me, but what it was, I had no idea. I was terrified of the unknown. Only time would tell and I feared the story it felt compelled to tell me.

Chapter Eight

WALKING OUT

PORT QUIN, CORNWALL, U.K.

AUGUST 6, 1841

I was so thankful to reach the safety of home that I walked through the house searching for my mother and then heartily embraced her. I found her caring for Moses in his little pen that Cade had built, as promised, next to the barn. The rain was now merely a light drizzle. She wore a knitted green triangular shawl over her head and upper body, the kind she sold in Port Isaac, which was the colour of newly grown leaves.

"I had a terrible fright walking by the graveyard, Mother, and I am so relieved to see you."

"Effy, child, all be well an' safe. What fright ails ye?" She looked at me with deep, concerned and pondering eyes.

"Just an imaginary scene of open graves. It's over now. How is Moses doing? Is he well? He looks so sweet and clean." I knelt and pulled him up and out of his pen. His little tail wagged wildly, and he licked my face.

"I gave him a bath and fed him, just like a wee babe," Mother said, beaming at us. "He has been a very good boy, and that's for sartin." She stroked his head.

I petted his curly white wool and felt so soothed by his softness. His warm little body was so in need of mothering and Mother and I were only too happy to give it.

"I'm meeting William after supper, and we are going walking at the Head. I have decided to walk out with William, Mother. I know Father won't approve but I hope you do. William is who I want in my future."

"William is a fine choice and make no mistake. T'es a good decision, Effy," Mother said, stroking my upper arm.

"Will you help me with Father, and convince him to let me walk out with William?" I asked, firmly. My tone said to her that I needed her support, and I knew she knew exactly what I meant, with no need for further words.

"Yes, steadfastly, even when 'es bin takin too much drink," she said, her lips closed firmly together, nodding her head.

I put Moses down in his pen and patted his head. He bleated in protest. We laughed at his pitiful little cries. I turned and gave Mother a firm embrace in gratitude. "Come and get out of this weather. I will help you get supper on the table."

After supper, Father was busy in the barn, so I slipped out when I saw William coming down the street to meet me. I silently darted out of the house and hurried along to greet his smiling face. I wore the only other day frock I owned which was a dark blue with a floral pattern and a stiff cream coloured lace border around the neckline that Gran had crocheted for me. My straw bonnet had several light blue paper flowers to the inside left corner, near my cheek, for adornment. He took stock of me.

"How are you, my lovely? You look the very same as this summer's eve. Warm, bright, and full of promise," he said, his eyes on mine and taking my hand, pulling me to him.

"Why thank you, kind sir," I replied. "I can't wait to be on the Head with you. My heart and mind feel full there."

With a grand gesture, putting my hand through his arm, he said, "Let's be off then."

We strode past the harbour where the fishing boats had been put to bed for the night. The weather had now brightened up and Mr. Tremaine, one of the fishermen I had seen at church, sat on the quay playing his fife. The sweet tune lifted in the warm breeze like the down of a thistle, lilting and rising over our heads and fading as we walked by. The Collins' children, all five of them, played marbles in the dirt next to the line of moored boats and shrieked in delight when one of them apparently won their game.

Samuel Collins, the oldest, sat on a rock ledge nearby, knitting. A stout boy of about twelve, he appeared from the look on his face with his tongue stuck out between his teeth and with notable holes in his work, that he was struggling with his knitting. He heaved a heavy sigh as he stuck a finger through one of the holes.

"What's the matter, Sam?" William asked, stopping as we walked by.

"Dunno. I done made holes of me stitches," he replied.

"Mum says I 'ave to make me own socks from now on."

"Let me take a look," William said, kneeling and examining the tangle of brown yarn. "Seems to me you are dropping the loop here, too early. I see many fine stitches in your work. Perhaps the holes are only mistakes that you can fix later. Such is life, you know, Sam. When you are learning, you make mistakes. We all do." William looked up at me. I nodded my head in agreement. Samuel looked at William with true appreciation and gratitude. "The main thing is to keep going. Keep trying. Everyone makes mistakes. The important thing is to learn from them and do the best we can." William tousled Samuel's brown hair with his fingers and stood back up, smiling. "There's a good lad. Run and find Henry. He's back at the house, which is a rarity. Usually, he is off fishing in one cove or another." Henry, also twelve, was William's only sibling, as apparently his mother had lost many young children due to influenza, according to my mother.

"Thanks, Willie. Maybe this be a glove an' I the hole for a finger!" Samuel said, laughing as we waved goodbye.

I admired William's patience and kindness with Samuel. "That was kind of you," I said, tucking my arm back into his.

"Making your own socks is tedious work as a child. No patience!" William joked, looking down at me. "The poor lad could use a hand, don't you think?"

"At the rate he's going, he might as well use what he's made as a minnow trap," I joked back.

"Oy! I can smell the remains of someone's supper. Roast pork, maybe?" he said, looking around us. The angles of his face reminded me of the ruggedness of the shoreline. His face was strong and resolute but his eyes, like the sea meeting the shore on a fine sunny day, exuded a calm depth that drew me in with their gentle allure. "Or is it pheasant?" He looked at me and licked his lips in the most wolfish way. I couldn't help but laugh at his surprising and out of character humor. William usually seemed fairly serious and reserved but I loved his humour and how it was spilling forth now that he was more comfortable around me.

"Nothing that lovely. Most likely rabbit. Whatever it is, it smells wonderful. I think it must be coming from Mrs. Rowe's kitchen. Perhaps I will ask her tomorrow what she made that smelled so good." I offered.

"And if she has any left-over!" William added, good-naturedly. "I always think with my stomach!" We giggled and held hands as we trudged up the path with the harbour and the boats on our left. Doyden Castle was coming into view behind them, as was Doyden Point beyond that across the water. As we climbed higher, the dramatic landscape before us seemed now to unfold in the most vast and dramatic way, even though we had seen it many times before. The narrow V shape of Port Quin was nestled in the rugged embrace of the coastline, as if carved by some ethereal sculptor.

"I never tire of the rocky cliffs, the sea, looking back inland towards Trelight Farm, my family, and friends, but I can't help but feel in my heart there must be something more to life than this poor seafaring existence. Weaving nets. Setting lobster pots. I know you feel the same." I murmured, feeling like he and I were kindred spirits.

"I do. I feel that way exactly when I am working on my boat building. I feel like my mind takes over and that I am destined to work in a bigger town," William said, threading his hand through his thick hair.

"I am truly grateful for all I have and I often feel guilty for wanting more. What I really want is to learn more about healing, as I told you before," I sighed. "I want to be more educated in healing. To help others."

"Healing others is next to godliness. But something seems to be bothering you from that sigh you just gave. What is it? Can you tell me?" His eyes were probing mine. I felt I had to tell him about Cade's proposal.

"Yes. Something has happened. With Cade." I paused.

William stopped walking and crossed his arms over his chest. "Go on," he said, gingerly.

"Cade plans to ask me to marry him, tomorrow I believe, and my father has agreed, without my permission. I am not accepting Cade, to be clear." I was completely relieved after this confession spewed out.

William's eyebrows knitted together. "I see. How do you feel about his intentions?" he asked seriously.

"At first I was flattered, but of course I would never agree to marry Cade. I am fond of him, as a childhood friend, of course, having grown up with him. But I would never marry him. Please know that. He has in no way touched my heart, no matter what he says." Even though I loved Cade in a different way and his handsome face and sensual body held a spell over me, I hoped my eyes would convey my true feelings for William that I myself was not ready to say to him.

"I believe you completely. And to be sure, I am happy that you will not accept him if he does ask you. But does he know this? He will not accept "no" for an answer easily, if I know Cade," William said, pressing his lips in consternation.

"No, he doesn't. Nor does my father," I said, forlornly, looking off into the distance.

William eyed me intently. "Effy, Cade is a man who wants what he can't have all the more because he can't have it. Does that make sense?"

"If you mean that he wants me only because I continue to put him off, then yes," I replied, somewhat guiltily, as I didn't like to string Cade, my long-time friend along like that.

"Not that I am perfect myself. I am not. I don't want you to think of me as someone who thinks I am perfect, because I don't. I have made mistakes. Have done things that I am not proud of," William said, putting his hands on his hips and looking out into the bay with a distant look on his face. "I have made very grave mistakes. Mistakes I will need to explain soon. Very soon."

"What could you have possibly done that is so wrong?" I asked, playfully, trying to get his happy mood to return. I reached out to his little finger and gave it a playful tug. He turned to me and smiled.

"Come, let us enjoy what short time is left in this day," he said lightly, wanting to change the subject. "I have special plans for us this evening. After a short visit to the cliffs, I want to show you our ship building workshop for a few minutes. My mother will be there, and we can show you around if you are keen?" He asked as if he doubted that I would want to see his ship building passion.

"Of course!" I was only too eager to see the secret goings on inside the Carlyon household.

As we neared the edge, the expanse of the bay came into view, its rough and uneven shore framed a churning sea that roared and crashed against unyielding rocks below. The waters, dark and tumultuous, mirrored in some regard the emotions that stirred in my soul. The elements seemed to evoke my sense of foreboding of secrets buried beneath the relentless tides. *No, not now,* I begged my mind. *No more visions of some dreadful thing.*

We ran up to the several large rocks on the cliffs and beheld the glory of Port Quin Bay. Our hands shielded our eyes from the brightness of the setting sun. The wind was whipping up the waves, their white tufted tips occasionally clapped together as their angles met sweeping and crashing on the craggy rocks below. Gulls looking for their next meal screeched and cawed overhead with their endless cries, some loud and some faded by the wind. We turned to each other, slightly out of breath from our running, and we soaked in not only the beauty from the fresh air and the open and wild scenery, but the natural beauty of each other.

I could only imagine what was going through his mind as we stood absorbing each other away from prying eyes. I took all of him in my mind and heart. His face was as chiseled as a rock face and he had a strong sense of self to match the cliffs as well. I could almost see his soul through his sensitive, intelligent eyes, whose kindness told me William would never hurt me. We grasped hands, his being strong and calloused, and I could feel his inner strength.

"Shall we sit for a few minutes?" He said, motioning us to a soft patch of grass.

"I would love nothing more," I smiled.

I was pulling my skirts about me when I felt that stirring feeling again. I felt compelled to look out in the water, not far from where we stood. Being with William out on the Head made my emotions surge and it was as if something was welling up inside me that I could not put aside. I looked out into the water but saw nothing unusual at first. I felt something urging me to look again. I saw a glimmer of something shiny. Just for an instant. A shiny glint out in the water caught my eye and then disappeared.

"What is it, Effy? Something in the water?" William stood back up and craned his neck in the direction I was looking.

"I thought I saw something. Just there. Past those crests and to the left…" I trailed off. " I saw something shiny. Like a shiny spark of something. Something is out there but I can't explain what." I said, pointing. "About the distance between your house to the port side cliffs," I explained, describing the location as best as I could.

"No. I don't see anything," William calmly replied. "Let me stand behind you and see exactly what you are seeing." He came and stood behind me, crouching down several inches so that his face was level to mine. He pressed his head against mine. I felt the most glorious sensation of love passing between us that I had ever felt in my life. The warmth of our heads touching, even though I had my bonnet on, was an unexpected connection. A warm gush of what I could only call deep, heartfelt love mixed with passion flared through my body.

"I don't see anything." He looked into my eyes and saw apparently saw my determination. "Was it a splash, from a fish? Or a fin, from a shark?"

"No, it wasn't a splash or a fin," I said in frustration trying to find a way to explain what I feared was a premonition without having to explain that I was seeing the black arts during our first time walking out. "I must have seen the sun shining against the water. But I know something is there."

Chapter Nine

Don't Tell a Soul

Port Quin, Cornwall, U.K.

August 6, 1841

"I am going in for a better look. Perhaps it was a mermaid," he said, with a brilliant, wry smile. In an instant, William stripped off his white shirt. Then he sat on the grass, ripping off his boots, and socks, against my protests.

"Is that a good idea? The waves? The rocks?" I faltered. I wasn't sure where my eyes should look, at his bare chest or out at the water.

"Bah, it's an easy swim. Only about ten yards! My curiosity is sparked now! I have a fishing knife here in my belt. Could be dinner of some kind! Or treasure!" His eyes were merry with excitement and suggested that a full-blooded pirate stood in front of me.

"But how will you get down and back up here safely?" I asked, looking over the steep edge of the cliff.

"Child's play, my lovely. No worries! Henry and I have been up and down these cliffs many times." And with that, he leaned down, his large hands gripping the larger of the boulders and he swung himself down, rock by rock and dove into an oncoming wave and disappeared beneath the surface as easily as a merman.

"I'm alright. You see?" He said, as he swam a few arm lengths toward the object. He popped his head up again. "Am I close to it?" William called out.

"A bit farther!" I called out, waving my hand and upper arm in case the wind took my words away. He waved an acknowledgement and then swam farther, arm over arm, as if the waves were no match for his strength.

I heaved a sigh of relief that no fearsome images had come to me and I continued to try to press them from my mind. *What was the matter with me?* My mind had become so dark and full of doom that I had begun to worry like an old woman. I saw Willam's pink feet up in the air as he dove down to the bottom at about the spot that seemed to call to me. He came to the surface and dove down several times. He managed the water with ease despite the undulation of the waves. I waited for what seemed like many minutes for him to resurface.

"I found it!" he yelled. Or I think that was what he yelled. The wind was blowing, and I had difficulty understanding him. His feet kicked and splashed as he went under again and again, searching around the place where I directed him. Each time, he drew in a deep breath and his legs kicked mightily, plunging him deep below the rolling surface of the water. Treading on the surface after several attempts, his search seemed to be completed. He began to swim back, with only one arm this time. His progress was slower. I went down as far as I could on the rocks but dared not go down as far as he did for fear of slipping and injuring myself on the steep drop to the water. I kept my eyes on him as he sputtered and thrashed through the waves, finally making his way back to shore. His chest was heaving from the exertion.

"I found something!" he called out, clearly out of breath and struggling to get back to shore.

"Focus on getting out of the water safely first." I chided him with a smile. He had something black under his arm that looked heavy. He heaved a black box onto a flat rock. The box was metal and rusted and about the length of my forearm and about five inches tall, I estimated. "What is that?" I asked, my eyes full of surprise.

William hoisted himself out of the water and onto the large, flat rock and flopped onto his back, breathing heavily. He wiped the drops off his face and slicked back his thick blond hair to get it out of his eyes. My own eyes were locked on the taut muscles of his chest and his rib cage, rising and falling with each breath and his trim waist and narrow hips. The way his muscular shoulders and chest glistened. I didn't even try to look away even though I knew I should. "That," he said triumphantly as he sat up in his wet trousers, "is a box from a paymaster's chest. My father has some of these chests. This is a smaller box that is part of a large chest. Used for carrying coins or for hiding jewelry in the larger chest."

I knew in an instant that this box was the very thing that I sensed in the water. I knew it like I knew the sun would rise tomorrow. I didn't know how I knew, but I knew it. "But that isn't shiny at all," I said, confused.

"No, but this is." He pulled a small silver coin out of his pocket that had a small corner of the silver showing through green algae which smothered the rest of the coin. How?" He panted. "How in God's name did you know this was there?" He looked at me with such disbelief and surprise. I knew I had to choose my words carefully.

"Honestly, I didn't know that was there at all. I saw a small glint of something shiny. I just had a feeling something was out there, William. I can't explain it. I could be nothing but an old box."

He thrust his hand deep into his pocket and pulled out four more silver coins that he held up for me to see as I was looking down at him from the rocks above. "I found five of these coins next to the box! You must have seen a shine off one of these, but I can't see how through the depth of the waves. Let me climb back up and I will show them to you."

"The tide is coming in. Please hurry." I said, pointing to the water rising around him on the rocks. He grabbed the box and stuffed the coins back into his pocket and began to discern a path back up the cliff.

"First, we must mark this spot in case we want to come back. To seek more treasure." He wiped his face and looked around for a way to mark the spot. But the rocks were slippery with algae and lined with treacherous mussels.

"There's no time! The sun is setting," I called. "The tide!"

"Do you have a petticoat we could rip? Anything?" William urged.

I looked about frantically. I untied my bonnet and slipped it off. I leaned over the cliff, bundled it up and tossed it to him. He struggled to get his footing and slipped several times.

Taking the bonnet, he wedged it in between two rocks and then covered it with another smaller rock so that it would not be obviously seen. Then he attempted to clamber away from the rising waves, gouged his shin on the rocks and a rivulet of blood streamed down his shin. Water splashed up as the waves grew higher, making matters worse.

"William, can you find a way? What can I do?" I asked, growing worried.

"Throw my shirt down to me and I will tie the box in it and around my waist. That way I will be able to use both hands to climb." He suggested.

"Yes. Good idea." I ran to get the shirt and tossed it to him, but the wind carried it further away from him than I had intended. *Idiot!* "I should have tied a knot in the shirt for weight before I threw it," I lamented.

"I can manage!" William yelled back, seeing the scolding I was giving myself. He set the box down and scampered over several feet to grab the shirt. The hungry waves reached for the box and lapped at it. For a moment, I thought the waves might be able to lift the box, but he was able to reach it in time. He created a satchel like noose for it and quickly tied it around his waist, tightly. With both hands free, he clawed at the earth and rock, gashing his knees and forearms. Climbing at a slant across the face of the cliff, he was able to finally reach the top. I ran over to him. His face was streaked with mud.

"Oh, William, I put you in jeopardy all over a few coins and a box," I lamented, stroking the hair out of his face. He wiped his dirty hands on his trousers, stood up and untied the shirt, which had ripped and was now stained green. We stood examining William's wounds and then the box. "Only scrapes," he said. We ran our fingers over the black edges and the lock. The metal was quite thick, and the locking mechanism was solid and impenetrable.

"Not to worry. Not at all. What is in this box could change our lives, you and I, Effy. Or it could be filled with sand. Either way, don't tell a soul about this box or the coins. Oh, and I also found this peculiar little teapot lid."

From his other trouser pocket, he produced the most extraordinary, small, round teapot lid with a scratched gold round ball on top. The lid was porcelain and painted purple with other pictures as well. I reached out and took it in my hand, marveling at it. "How beautiful!" I exclaimed. He took it back into the safety of his own pocket.

"Could be more out there and maybe the pot to this! Come. We must go home and see my mother. And change out of these wet clothes!" He laughed. Blood ran down his calf, but he gave the trickle only the briefest glance. His face had a seriousness, an intensity, I had never seen. He knew something about this box and whatever was inside had an element of danger about it, to be sure.

Again, he insisted we mark the spot where we first stood and saw the flash in the water. "I don't have anything to mark the spot with except the blood from my shin," he said, looking up at me, laughing. He wiped the nearest rock with his bloodied hand, enough to smear the rock.

"Won't that arouse suspicion?" I asked.

"Around here? Just evidence of a good fight," he replied with a rakish grin. "I will come back later and properly mark the spot."

He held my hand as we practically ran down the hill and

to the left to get to the path towards the houses on the hill above Port Quin where he lived with his parents and Henry. The Carlyon home was a two-story white stone house, one of the better sort in Port Quin. The rumor was that their seeming wealth came from pirate treasure or more likely smuggling and that Mr. Carlyon was often not home because he was in prison for it. I was about to learn that nothing was farther from the truth.

We entered the back of the house closest to the Head by the kitchen, where Mrs. Carlyon was seated reading a large book at a table in front of the fire. She looked up calmly as we entered the room and eyed William's wet hair and clothes. She said nothing; her large eyes seemed to ask the necessary questions. William went to her, bent down, and kissed her cheek and said, "Mother, you remember Effy?"

Anne Carlyon was a calm, learned sort of woman. Her pale white skin lent her the appearance of someone who did not spend much time outside. She put down her book and reached out her hand to me. "Effy. How lovely to see you, my dear. How are you?"

"Quite well, Mrs. Carlyon. Lovely to see you as well." I cleared my throat as I clasped her hand in mine.

"Mother, we have something incredible to show you," William interjected, excitedly. " Effy found this in the water, just off Kellan Head. Please, have a look." William thrust the box, the five coins that he had found altogether and the tea pot lid from his pockets onto the table. "Mother is quite knowledgeable about old things," William said, looking at me and nodding in his mother's direction.

"Heavenly days!" Mrs. Carlyon whispered as her long

fingers slid over the black metal box. "Part of a paymaster's chest!" She lifted the box up, examining the lock. William and I exchanged anxious glances. The metal box dripped on the table.

She squinted at the box. "No markings but I would say the box itself is Spanish by the look of it. The larger box that this belongs to was probably a treasure in and of itself. Most likely seventy years old at least is my guess…" She trailed off. "Could be from one of the wrecks from 1807. There were three that Mr. Trevan wrote about in his book from 1835 that I have read and taken notes from, which contain a record of all the wrecks in the parish from 1800 to 1835. And of course, there were many. One of those wrecks was the ship the *Nervy* from London to Cork carrying two thousand barrels of butter that went over in a hurricane near here. A large load like that would likely have a large paymaster's box, perhaps with a smaller box for coins and jewels like this one. What better way to hide a secret trove than in a humble shipment of butter!" She quipped.

"Can you get it open?" William asked, impatiently. I stood motionless, taking in the scene. I did not know Mrs. Carlyon well, but I was immediately impressed by her apparent knowledge. I had never known anyone like her. She and her son both mesmerized me. He had something of her depth of calm and had her same resolute facial features.

Her maid, Hannah, a stout young girl with dark hair and several missing teeth, passed through the kitchen with a tray of dishes from the dining room. "Evenin' Will, Miss," she nodded to us as she walked by to the wash tub in the adjacent scullery. I knew that Anne, even though she was not an old woman, had pain in her back and hips and walked with an awkward gait, as if her back was crooked. Apparently Hannah was there to help with household chores to reduce Anne's workload. I didn't know Hannah well but had seen her at chapel in town for years with her large and family who often came threadbare and thin. I thought it was good of Anne to take her in and provide Hannah with work which she and so many others like her needed.

"Difficult to say" Anne said in a whisper. "We can try the keys we have from similar boxes, but I doubt they will open it," she mused, putting the box down on the table and turning to the coins. "Hannah," Anne called out to the scullery. "That will be all for today, dear. Thank you." Anne looked at William and I sternly. We took her meaning and said no more until Hannah came back through the main kitchen and had closed the door behind her. We waited until we saw her walk down the path through the window. Anne nodded. Only then did she continue. "The coins date back to 1722. Spanish. Very valuable. What else did you see at this site, William?"

"Found this teapot lid," he said, pointing to it on the table. "I didn't look for anything more. I was too busy with the box, the coins, and the rising tide to be honest." He shrugged.

"Did you mark the site?" Anne asked, one eyebrow arched.

"Of course, Mother," William quickly replied.

"Good. But first, William, go and put on some dry trousers, and perhaps a shirt?" She motioned to him with her hand to be off.

I thought to add, "And wash off those scrapes with soap and clean water."

William nodded and turned to dash off to the stairs,

presumably to his bedroom. "Right. Back directly."

"Effy, would you like some tea?" Mrs. Carlyon asked.

I shook my head. "Oh, no, thank you. I believe I am too excited about this find at the moment. And I must be getting back home soon. But I am curious about the book you are reading. What is it, if I may ask, and where did you find it?"

"Oh, this?" She replied, looking down fondly at the book and gently slid it over to me. "Yes, it was a gift from my husband, Charles, from a recent trip to London. I have been using it for our ship building, you see."

I gently took the book as she slit it across the table to me, careful to not lose her place. The book was filled with glorious sketches of a variety of vessels drawn in parts with great attention to detail, from the mast to the keel. "How have you learned...?" I questioned, my jaw dropping, I was so impressed, as I waved my hand over the drawings.

"Bit by bit, day by day, over many years. You can do the same. I can give you a book to study if you like..." I felt daunted inside by her accomplishments and wondered if I could truly do the same. I marveled over both her manner and her intelligence.

I flipped through several more pages of the book. "Have you actually been to London?" I asked, sliding the book back to her.

"Yes, several times," Anne replied slowly, smiling at my intrigue.

"What was it like? Really like? I've heard a great many things." I leaned forward onto the table.

"Magical!" Anne said, her eyes gleaming.

"Mother, if we could. How can we open the box now,

please?" William entered the room quickly and circled the table behind Anne and placed his hands on her shoulders. "I could get a hammer and break it open," he said, looking down at her.

She turned over her shoulder, startled, and said, "Not on your life! You would damage what is inside. Think, my child. The tumblers! We must think about the locking mechanism. We need to find a tool in the workshop. And only open this box in complete secrecy."

Chapter Ten

An Ominous Knock

Port Quin, Cornwall, U.K.

August 6, 1841

Anne pushed back from the kitchen table, and we walked back through the kitchen door and outside to our immediate left and into a small outbuilding, larger than the kitchen but smaller than the house, which served as the boat building workshop. "We built this shed on the side of the cliff, as you can see," William explained, "so that we can hoist finished vessels over the side on pulleys, down the cliff and into the water. The whole job needs care but works quite well," he said.

"Ingenious," I marveled, looking around the side of the building to just get a glimpse of some of the gear and portions of hulls awaiting completion and swinging over the side of the cliff.

William looked back at me and smiled as he opened the lock on the thick door and held it open for his mother and I to enter.

Inside, the first thing I noticed was the distinctive smell of wood, sawdust, and tar lingering in the air. The space was cluttered and filled with an assortment of tools, materials, and drawings. In the middle, a sturdy, thick workbench was scarred with marks and grooves from past jobs. I looked around in complete amazement. The walls were covered with neatly drawn plans for trading vessels, much larger than could be built or launched in Port Quin. I could identify a few drawings as schooners from the multiple masts, or as brigs with square-rigged sails, and large cargo holds. Next to these drawn plans were others for fishing boats, with their net storage and space for storing the catch. Each plan had its own unique proportions detailed out with lines, figures, and angles drawn. I was captivated by the sheer display of ability that I saw before me. Questions swirled around in my mind as to who had made these plans and who would take them off the paper and turn them into reality.

William asked, pointing to the array on the workbench," Do you recognize these tools, Effy?"

"Let me see. Mallet, yes. Hand saw, yes." William went to the bench and picked up the tools one by one for me to identify. "That one is...I don't know that one," I laughed.

He held up a flat bottomed, rectangular tool. "A hand plane," he answered. "Used for shaping and smoothing wood surfaces.

"William, this is all so masterful. Who created these brilliant plans?" I asked, truly in awe.

"The family Carlyon!" He exclaimed, putting a hand to his heart, proudly. "Our family business in its infancy. We plan

someday to build merchant ships, but possibly cutters and luggers first. If all goes well and the demand for vessels of all
kinds increases as we believe it should, then we may expand
to schooners as we build for our customers. Father is in London securing capital now. We do all this work together."

William lit two lanterns, one for me and one for him and
his mother. The two of them looked through the drawers in
an old chest in search of a key or a tool to open the box while
I looked at several old maps and took in the atmosphere of the
workshop. This space, the birthplace of voyages to come lo-
cated in the heart of Cornwall's maritime legacy, exuded an
aura of craftsmanship that whispered tales of seafaring lore to
come. The room bore the marks of countless hours spent hon-
ing the art of shipbuilding, its very walls imbued with the salt
from the wisdom of tireless devotion to the sea. To me, the
tools lay as silent witnesses to the hopes and dreams of the
Carlyon family to make a better life for themselves through
their own ingenuity and handiwork. The hand planes, their
wooden handles worn smooth by countless passes over unyielding timber held the promise of shaping dreams into vessels that could brave the roughest sea, and the vessels would
deliver the Carlyons to the distant shore of prosperity. I could
see it all so clearly now. Mr. Carlyon was no smuggler.

Suddenly, a loud, ominous knock banged on the front door
of the main house. Our heads all jerked towards the direction
of the harsh knocking. "Hallo to the house? Anyone about?" A
loud and gruff male voice called out.

William looked at me in complete shock. "It's Cade!" He
said in a low hiss. William's face told me he knew how much
trouble Cade could be, especially given Cade's recent interest

in me. Serious trouble.

Anne looked at us in alarm and said, just above a whisper, "He sounds angry."

William answered, "Yes, I daresay this isn't a social call."

"He must know I'm here. My father won't approve. Cade will tell him! I whispered in a panic, my voice trembling.

"Quickly! Run! Back to the kitchen." William took his mother by the arm. She winced at being forced to stand so quickly. We ran out of the workshop door, Anne with difficulty, and through the open kitchen door. "If anything should happen to me, this treasure belongs to Effy. Do you hear me, Mother?"

"Yes, but…" was all she could get out as she whispered back, her head cocked to the side in question as she slid back into her chair.

William took me by the upper arms, gripping me tightly. "Effy, my love, run. Run out this door and around the back of the house. Run as quickly and silently as you can." With that, he kissed me fully and warmly on the lips sending a jolt of passion through my body and he forcefully pushed me towards the door and turned to walk to the front of the kitchen, blocking the view of the kitchen door through which I was so suddenly leaving.

"Cade, come in. Oh, I see you already have." William said loudly.

"William. Mrs. Carlyon. Good evening." Cade's voice rang out.

"Evening, Cade." I heard Mrs. Carlyon say in her typical calm voice as I rounded the kitchen wall outside.

"What brings you here, Cade? A strange time of evening

for a call. Looking for company at the inn?" William said, his back to the kitchen wall now, blocking the window I was passing outside.

"Not this time, Willy. I'm looking for Effy. Is she here?" Cade spoke with a heated, terse tone.

I ran. I ran with my skirts in my hands down the harbour path, avoiding the inn and went on the path and around Quay Street, to the other side of the harbour and home. As I approached home, I slowed my steps and my breathing before entering.

I realized I didn't have my bonnet as I was collecting my thoughts before I opened the door. Just as I pulled the door open, my father walked through the room, his boots thudding loudly on the floor. He looked tired but his appearance was neat and orderly. I looked around for Mother, but she was nowhere to be seen.

"Where ye been?" he barked. "No bonnet. No scarf. I'll 'ave none of yer rudeness."

I thought quickly. I am a grown woman. I refused to lie about William. "I was walking with William and went to his house to see his mother. They have the most interesting ship building workshop..."

"Walkin' out with William Carlyon? Did I give permission? Wasn't ye s'posed to meet Cade?" He began to rant.

"No, you did not give permission, Father, but..." In an instant his coarse, rough hands were around my throat, and he backed me up against the wall by the front door. His hands constricted my breathing. I was stunned and couldn't move. I was shocked but not completely surprised given how short tempered my father was. Now I knew the seriousness of

Cade's interest. The back of my head began to hurt as he pressed it painfully against the stones of the wall.

His face was close to mine. "No, I ain't gave no permission. I ain't dun dat. You ain't walkin' out with dat foul pirate's son, William. Ye'll go with Cade. Do ye understand? Do ye understand? Do ye understand me?" He screamed and throttled my neck at the same time. I felt full of shame. My hands hung at my sides. I was painfully embarrassed by what my father was doing to me as an adult, as his daughter. Why would he do such a hateful thing? Tears welled up in my eyes uncontrollably. What had I done to deserve this? I felt so lowly and despised by my own father, my family. Where was my mother? Surely she had heard this.

"Yes, I understand you," I said, and the hands that were shackles released me and Father walked away. I stroked my neck for a few moments and fought back hot tears that rolled down my cheeks. The idea to fight against him never occurred to me simply because he was my own father. He was the head of the household—to be respected. Dazed, I went to my bedroom to lick my wounds and prayed that sleep would take me away to a better world.

Chapter Eleven

A Nasty Scar

August 7, 1841

The next morning, I awoke to my mother screaming. I ran out of my bedroom, frantically searching for her, praying that my father hadn't done something horrid to her like he had done to me. I found her outside by Moses' pen, pointing, her hand over her mouth. I looked where she was pointing. There in his pen lay my poor little lamb, Moses, his pink tongue hanging out of his mouth in a pool of his own blood, a wide slit down his belly with his entrails hanging out. He was dead.

The sight of his white wool soaked with blood was so devastating, so cruel, that my spirit was instantly crushed. I sank to my knees beside him. His pure white fleece, once a testament to innocence, was now stained with the sticky crimson liquid of his tragic end. His gentle body, once so bouncy and full of joy to see me, now lay limp and gutted like a stray fish by a malicious hand. My heart bled inside with a grief and a hatred that clawed at the depths of my being. Who would do such a hateful thing to such a harmless creature? I felt my mouth open and shut several times with nothing coming out. Mother tried to console me but I took little notice.

Anguish washed over me like a wave that threatened to pulverize me on the sand and drag me across the sea floor. Tears flowed down my cheeks, not just from sorrow, but from rage. A fire within me burned at the injustice of this crime that was obviously aimed at me, besides being a wanton slaughter of a harmless, sweet lamb! The killing was someone's need to prove their power over me, and the thought of the cruelty against a humble lamb because of me, because of some un-known action on my part, was unbearable. What could I have done to cause such a cruel reaction?

I felt my eyes burning with a fierce intensity, promising retribution to the unknown perpetrator of this vicious crime against the lamb and to me. My mind became a tempest and every breath I took became more and more ferocious. The winds around us mourned with me and began to whip and whirl across the quay. The moor agreed with my anguish and echoed my pain through its undulating hillside. I vowed to seek the truth, to unveil the vile soul who committed this act and had stolen my beloved Moses away. I would become a force to be reckoned with. And I knew where to start.

I wiped my cheeks with the back of my hands. I would make that someone feel what I felt. I stretched out my arm and put my palm in the pool of Moses' blood.

I went into my parents' bedroom where Father was wash-ing his face and thick beard, making ready for his day on the

Mary. I held up my palm to his back as he faced the cloudy mirror, soap in his powerful, strong hand. Blood dripped down my palm onto my arm and splattered onto the floor.

"Saints alive. What the 'ell, Effy?" Father yelped, turning, and yanking his body to step aside.

"Did you do this?" I asked him, calmly and plainly, my feet spread apart and my knees locked. He stared at me blankly.

"What the bloody 'ell ye on about? Effing 'ell!" His mouth hung open as he looked at my palm.

"Did you kill Moses, my lamb, you bastard?" I screamed at him. He dropped the soap on the floor.

"No, I ain't killed no lamb! What da 'ell are ye on about? Jesus, ye got the blood from it?" The soap dripped from his thick beard onto the floor.

Of course, I didn't believe him. He and I stood glaring at each other at a precipice. My heart was ablaze with an anger that consumed me, and I assumed the raging flames flared across my face, striking out at him. My once innocent features were now contorted with a furious resolve that I felt inside toward my menacing father. My lamb Moses, my gentle new companion whom I had hoped would bring me comfort in a bleak and lonely existence, lay butchered. I could not escape the cruel visions of my father's strong and wicked hand holding the fisherman's knife that cut through his soft flesh like butter. I knew and saw in my mind that Moses ran up to Father willingly, wanting a good ear scratching. Did Moses kick and struggle? I couldn't get the images out of my mind.

Usually, my father's gaze, cold and penetrating, pierced through me and caused me to shrink back in fear. But I had had enough of this fear. More than enough! I was tired of the shame he brought on me and my mother, with the drawings of nude women in lewd acts that I often found sticking out of his side of the mattress while I cleaned their room, and especially what I saw with Cornelia. I thought of the years' worth of indiscreet sounds my father made during "the act" and me growing up with my pillow over my head in what seemed like a nightly occurrence. My poor mother was always silent. Inwardly, I was tired of my own silence and had become less fragile, stronger, as if I had nothing left to lose. My silence and my anger, like the relentless gusts that swept across the desolate moor, could no longer be contained.

"I demand an answer. Who slit Moses, the lamb, wide open, and left him to die in his pen? Was it you?" I asked, confronting him again, knowing full well he could strike me down if he wanted, being the twisted man that he was.

"Demands, is it? Ye're makin' demands o' me?" He asked, grabbing a towel of a hook and wiping his face with quick, rugged swipes. "I is the one in this house that makes demands, Effy," he said, calmly this time. I stood my ground, knowing full well he would likely reach out and slap me. "That's for sartin. And 'ere's what's to be done. You is to leave this house and not come back. Ye understand? Now ye've got to git some udder place to live. Ye ain't welcome 'ere no more," he sneered.

He came up close to my face, nodding in a sick way, trying to terrorize me with his every word. I smelled the perfumed scent of the soap but thought all the while about how much my father stank with his lack of integrity. I treaded that thin line between love and loathing, bound by the ties of blood. But blood didn't protect me now. My spirit was wounded deep down, but on the surface it propelled me forward, urging me to finally face the shadows that my mother and I had cowered for years. At that moment, my anger collided with the shadows, unlocked the vault that held these secrets, and opened my heart to forge a path of my own, finally lightening this wretched burden.

"With pleasure," I said, pausing afterward to make sure he heard me fully and that he realized that I was not saddened by his proposal for one second. His face was completely blank, which was fine by me. I turned and walked out of the house.

Dr. Moyle and I sat in the surgery that morning, as it was my day to assist. I was more than happy to recover from the incident with Father in the sanctity of the consulting room with Dr. Moyle, one of the most rational and kind men I knew. I had thought about Father's words. *No matter. I would live with Gran until I could sort something different and permanent out. Mother would be close by. All would be well,* I told myself. Work with Dr. Moyle was a source of happy continuity without worry about emotional confrontations or the need to walk on hot stones. His demeanor was always the same: happy, professional, productive, all of which calmed my frayed nerves.

As promised, Dr. Moyle taught me about bones and fractures that day to increase my ability to respond to the medical needs in Port Quin.

"Now, Effy, what are the symptoms of a fracture, as we discussed, versus the symptoms of bruising or a sprain?" Dr. Moyle looked at me with his wrinkled brow as we reviewed several drawings of a femur bone.

"A fracture happens during the injury when the patient hears a crack or snap. The site then swells, bruises black and purple, and the pain is excruciating. If the bone comes through the skin, it is called an 'open' fracture."

"Yes, now please draw what you just described on this page," Dr. Moyle requested. "Keep in mind, the better you do, the more we can serve and the more we can charge." I looked up from my work briefly expecting to see humor in his eyes but instead I saw that strange stare again, as if he was sizing up my worth. I took it to mean his troubles with lack of payments at the surgery were mounting.

Someone came in just then; but, Dr. Moyle and I had our heads bent in concentration on my drawing and we barely noticed.

"Beggin' yer pardon," said Mr. Hawkins, the grain miller said frantically. "Sorry to disturb. I am looking for my dattur, Cornelia. Ain't no body seed her since last night. Have you seed her?" he asked, cautiously.

Dr. Moyle and I exchanged glances and then looked back at Mr. Hawkins. Dr. Moyle said, shaking his head, "I haven't seen your daughter. Was she ill, or was she with someone? Do you know the circumstances of when or where she was last seen, Mr. Hawkins?"

At the mention of Cornelia, my mind flashed back to the searing memory of her and my father in the barn and the gold chain on her wrist. I wonder how she explained where she got that to her own father. She might be with my father again or perhaps some other man. I looked down into my lap and blinked my eyes hard to push that nightmare of a memory far back into the recesses of my mind.

"Ma and me seed her at supper, and then she gone to the harbour an' seed a friend. That's all she said. We are quite worrit, ye see."

"Of course, you are. We'll ask in the village and keep a look out for her," I said, calmly. "She may have fallen asleep at a friend's house, is all." I tried to ease his fear. Clearly, her father was worried beyond measure.

"Alert the authorities if she is not found within a few hours," Dr. Moyle recommended with a serious tone.

"I done that." With that Mr. Hawkins lifted his hat and went on his way.

"How alarming," I said to Dr. Moyle in a fearful tone after Mr. Hawkins had gone.

"Yes," he agreed. "When a young woman goes missing, it is right to be concerned. But let's continue our drawing of the fracture for now if you please."

I drew the open fracture and Dr. Moyle commended my work. We discussed rotational fractures, and I also drew an example of that.

"The key to repairing an open wound is cleaning any debris from the area and cleansing it with alcohol, even whiskey or brandy, if you have that. Do you understand?" he asked.

Just then, the door burst open and Cade staggered in, clutching his left thigh. His right hand was bloodied.

"Good heavens!" I exclaimed.

"Get clean water, bandages, and the alcohol, Effy." Dr. Moyle calmly advised, taking one look at Cade's condition. Our book lesson was turning into a real-life example. I ran to the cupboard to get the supplies while Dr. Moyle helped Cade lie down on the examining table towards the back of the surgery.

"He knifed me!" Cade said.

"Who?" I exclaimed as Dr. Moyle and I cut away Cade's trousers and cleaned the blood away from the wound.

"Looks to be about two inches long and below the skin but not into the muscle," Dr. Moyle said, leaning down towards Cade's thigh to examine the damage. "Bite down on this, Caden. Effy, what do you think of the wound?" He gave Cade a thick pad of cloth to bite down on. Cade stuffed the cloth in his mouth, and he held on to the sides of the table. Dr. Moyle poured alcohol over the cut. Cade's eyes squinted in pain and he grimaced but made no sound. He did grab my hand for comfort, and I obliged.

"A clean cut that should be able to close up quickly but will leave a nasty scar," I said, applying pressure with a bandage. With the bleeding stopped, Dr. Moyle and I bound up the wound and Cade sat back up.

"You'll be a bit sore for a couple of weeks. Come see me in a few days so we can be sure the wound is not inflamed." He patted Cade's shoulder a few times and walked out the back door to wash his hands in the clean water.

I couldn't help but notice how stoically Cade handled the bleeding and the pain. "Now, what is this all about? Who did this?" I asked. Cade hesitated. "Who?" I asked again.

Cade's eyes shifted slightly. "William. He up and stabbed me this morning. We were arguing about you being there last night. He told me you were. First, he shoved me to the ground, unexpectedly. When I got up, he whipped out his knife and sliced me across the thigh," Cade explained, bitterness written across his face.

"What? That doesn't sound like William?" I was very confused over what I had just heard.

"Got me when I was down. Not very honourable, I would say," Cade said. He looked at me with such sincerity that I took in his story, almost believing it. He was persuasive in not only what he said but how he said it.

"But why the fighting? Why the knife? I don't rightly understand..." I trailed off.

"You. You are the reason. I want you to be my wife..." He began to say, but Dr. Moyle came in the door, clearing his throat.

"We will talk about this later," I whispered back to Cade. "Best be off home to recover now. Take this mint tea to help you relax and stay off your feet for at least the rest of today," I admonished.

"Can't. A school of herring has been sighted off the point. All the seamen of the village are making ready at this very moment to set sail. I'll take my leave to join my crew on the *Star*. We'll be cuttin' the ham tonight!"

"Well, we wish you good fishing then. Keep the wound dry," Dr. Moyle warned, his eyebrows sternly knitted together, as he busied himself with cleaning up.

I thought of protesting against Cade about going out with the fishermen but knew it would not be of much use. "Cade, you really shouldn't go. The wound could open and become worse."

"So, you do care for me after all." Cade smiled as his usually dashing figure limped over to the front door and swung it wide open. He leaned on it with his large, angular upper body, his eyes aflame with a wild and reckless fire. He reached out for my hand and pulled me toward him in one sweeping motion, suggesting our lips would meet. I needed to put him off but was afraid he would retaliate with my father again. I wanted to tell him then and there that I wanted to walk out with William. But I hesitated.

"Effy." When he spoke my name, the word rang inside my head with a tantalizing allure, a seductive magnetism. "I'll be gone, but when I return, I expect you to be by my side and to be in your arms. You will be in my thoughts." My heart started beating quickly in anticipation, but instead of any embrace, he released me quickly and said, "I'm coming back for you."

Once more, he had me torn between caution and uncertainty, like a wave crashing on the shore, and then running back to the sea, defying all the reasons I had used to decide my future. Try as I might to cut myself loose from him, I had some kind of flaw, a perpetual weakness, which kept me coming back to him again and again.

With some difficulty, I went back with Dr. Moyle to work beyond drawings of broken bones to actually practise bracing and bandaging on a sewn stuffed set of legs I had made myself, of which Dr. Moyle was very proud. He claimed they were very lifelike, not only in their size in shape, but because I had also included tree branches inside to represent bones that could be intact or "broken."

"Curious thing, that thigh wound on the young man, Caden," Dr. Moyle mused, looking at my work.

I looked up as I finished up the bandaging. "Oh, in what way?" I asked, unconcerned.

"The angle. Did you notice? The angle of the cut was such that it would have been done from right to left, rather than left to right as I overheard him describe to you." Dr. Moyle looked at me with a knowing glance. He knew exactly what he was saying but it took a few seconds for this to sink in for me. "Ah well, who will really know the truth in how the wound got there to begin with?" Dr. Moyle mused.

"I don't take your meaning," I stammered. Confused, I said, "Did he describe it in detail?"

"Yes, he did. Well. As I said. We will never know," he muttered, looking over my work.

"You are saying it is possible that the wound was self-inflicted," I replied, forcing calm into my voice.

"I am saying it is possible," he replied with a dark, brooding look in his eyes.

Chapter Twelve

A Party at Doyden Castle

Port Quin, Cornwall, U.K.

August 7, 1841

After a long and taxing morning, Dr. Moyle was called away on an errand and therefore asked if I could take care of cleaning up and locking of the surgery in the afternoon. I was sweeping up with quite a heavy heart and heavy thoughts when a young man knocked on the door. Since I was only a few minutes from locking up, I hesitated to open it, but duty called.

"Ye've got to come quick. A man up at the castle been shot and may be dead. We dunno. Can ye come?" he said.

"A man? Shot by a gun? That requires Dr. Moyle, but he has left on an errand. You must find him."

"No, Miss. Ain't no time. He ain't home. We done went there. Ye've got to come now, please."

"Very well. Let me fetch my bag and cloak," I said as I ran

to pack a few bandages and some salve in a satchel and grabbed my cloak, bonnet, and the key. "Who is this man?" I asked, quickly locking the door.

"Dunno his name. A gent from London, I s'pose. Quick, I'll help you up in the carriage. Name's Tom. I drive for Mr. Symons."

"A carriage?" I asked, in disbelief.

"Yes, Miss. Get in! We must hurry! I 'ave me orders." Tom replied, all business as he quickly took my hand and opened the door to the carriage. I sat inside the carriage-my first carriage ride-and I was aghast at the opulence inside. The interior was a light maroon brocade with tassels from the seat cushions that hung down. The backs of the seats were made of a fine, dark leather that held me in sumptuous comfort. The carriage could seat six comfortably, and with the extra room I bounced and jostled about inside it even as I held tightly to the passenger straps as the horses raced at top speed. We hurtled down the lane, past the church and around the harbour.

I began to have the most peculiar feeling. Amidst the carriage's rumbling wheels and thundering hooves, I heard the roar of waves, thundering down, causing great gushes of splashing water. I could hear and almost feel water roaring at me in all directions, but there was none in the carriage, of course. From the small carriage window, I could see the waves in the bay were rolling in with the usual look of the tide. All the fishing fleet were gone, as Cade had said they would be, gone after the shoal of herring. I craned my neck and saw that my father's boat, the *Mary*, was gone and even William's boat, the *Hope*, was gone as well. Nothing was amiss except that thick black clouds were forming over the horizon.

Another of my premonitions was coming, I thought to my-self with alarm. Waves and black clouds with the whole fleet out. Something ominous was about to happen, I could feel it. That same pulling feeling of terrible loss flooded over me with the gush of huge waves, the sound of crashing crests. Given the strength of the feeling and the sounds in my head, it seemed something would happen today, or soon. I began to tremble. I would get to the castle and return as quickly as pos-sible to warn the women of the village if the premonitions per-sisted. *But warn them of what? Waves?* Would they dismiss me as some had dismissed my grandmother in years past? As a lunatic? Or would they revere me as many had, seeing me as a woman steeped in the dark arts?

All the sudden, I began to feel very nauseous, either from the bumpy carriage ride or the feeling of waves in my mind. My stomach tightened and lurched. I felt the contents of my stomach pitch forward and I tried to hold it all in. I was afraid I would be sick inside the beautiful carriage. I tried to look at the horizon to reduce the nausea. But it was no use. I knocked with my fist on the ceiling of the carriage as hard as I could.

"Tom! Tom! I am sick! Stop the carriage!" I went to beat on the ceiling again but it was too late. I hung my head out of the window and vomited down the outside of the door.

"Wha?" Tom called as his head craned around to see me wiping my mouth on my sleeve and the ooze dripping down the side of his carriage. He slowed the horses.

"Now 'e've done it! I'll be in me grave if the master sees dat," he said, his nose crinkling up at the smell.

I had lunged out of the door and out on the road and stum-bled toward the grass. My stomach was in a terrible upheaval as was my mind. I stood at the edge of the road, on the cliff's edge, trying to catch my breath. The wind pulled at my scarf and hair and the clouds were the most peculiar shade of black I had ever seen during the day. I leaned over the cliff and spat out the bitter taste in my mouth.

What I saw then in the water below truly unnerved me. Below me, just beyond a large set of rocks, was the strangest thing I had ever seen. An image rippling on the water's surface. The image I saw was a reflection—so strange it took my breath away and made my knees weaken. The image was not a reflection of me staring down into the water. The image I saw was of myself, laying across my grandmother's lap, in what looked like complete despair. My hand was limp and hanging over my family's bible as Gran tried to comfort me. I stared at it and blinked. The image was colourful and clear— my Gran's white cap, the creamy pages of the bible, the blue sky out of the windows behind me. What it meant was not clear at all. I heard Tom's heavy boots tramp up behind me.

"There's no' swacks of time. We got to git going now. Storm be comin.'" Tom chided me to get back in the carriage.

"Do you see that there, in the water? I asked pointing to the image of myself in the water.

He looked where I was pointing. "I ain't seed nothin.' Now, back in the carriage wit 'e." I looked back at the water. The image was gone. My sickness vanished; I slowly pulled my scarf up around my head.

The carriage veered around the harbour and up the other side on the south cliff towards Doyden Castle. I had heard about the castle but had never been in it or even close to it. I decided it was a peculiar-looking castle, as it was small, but its ancient stones had an imposing presence all the same. The round tower loomed before me like a sentinel of ill begotten secrets, its large windows darkened like vacant eyes staring at me with an eerie foreboding that gripped me with fear. William had warned me not to go to the castle alone. *But surely during the day and to tend to an injured man, I must go, mustn't I?* I mustered my courage for the patient, whom I thought must be frightened as well.

As Tom and I entered through the castle's imposing black gates, he abruptly took his leave to continue with his carriage duties.

"Knock on the door straight 'way and the matron will show 'e where to go," Tom said, looking down at the horses' reins, avoiding my eyes.

I walked up the large and adorned stone staircase, reached out, and grasped the old, round, iron door knocker. The touch sent a shiver coursing through me as if an icy winter blast had blown right through me. The castle seemed to have a ghostly breath of tragedy to it, and I almost ran back to the path leading up to the gate. But I thought about my duty and waited. A heavy looking matron who seemed as if she never had a dream in her life opened the door and showed me in. She was heavy set, with meaty jowls, and she was dressed in a blue frumpy day gown that seemed overly fancy for her position.

Each step I took inside the dark castle corridors only added to my trepidation. The echoes of our footfalls were the only sounds about except the faint whispers from dark corners of conversations long past. Shadows danced on fancy looking tapestries of wild hunting scenes and lush crimson draperies with gold tassels. Enormous paintings from floor to ceiling flagrantly depicting nude women and men in various forms of celebrations hung from gilded gold frames. Grotesquely ornate wall sconces held tall candles that had largely burned out and needed attention; their melted wax had fallen on the floor. Stains covered the thick garishly coloured carpets. The atmosphere was an odd mixture of perverse gaiety and a warped reality, and I wondered who could possibly call this strange place home. I clung to my cloak and my breath in awe and dread of what was to come.

"Where is the injured man? Are you taking me to him now?" I asked her.

"Yes, Miss. Just through 'ere," she said, her gravelly voice echoing in the large corridor.

I was intrigued by the castle but I also had concerns that began ringing in my ears. One was about the wounded man and what I could possibly do for him. As I followed the matron, I tried to focus on the steps Dr. Moyle would take to evaluate the man's condition and what course of action he would follow. *Evaluate gunshot entry and exit, clean the wounds, stop any bleeding if possible, ease shock by keeping the patient warm...* But since the matron didn't seem overly concerned, was there even a wounded man? Was she that callous that she didn't care that a man lay dying? Or was I walking into some kind of trap? She didn't seem the least bit concerned about me either, so I didn't know what to believe.

She reached for a doorknob and opened it with a pudgy fist and urged me to go through with a nod of her head. In the dim light, I saw several fancy gowns hanging in an open wardrobe. "What is this?" I asked, confused.

"The master don't allow guests in 'ere without proper

attire. He asks that ye change into something more fittin'." She grabbed the first garments she could reach off the rack and thrust them towards me—a pink long sleeved blouse and voluminous white skirt.

"I prefer to wear my own clothes, thank you kindly," I said, holding the skirt and blouse out to her.

"Ye will wear it. The master insists," she barked.

"Very well, since time is critical for the injured man. If I must." I reluctantly went behind a silk screen and put on the skirt and blouse that the matron forced me to wear. The blouse was much more tight fitting than I would ever think of wearing. *Ridiculous*, I thought. I hung my own blue frock on top of the screen. She snatched it down with a *snap*.

"I might as well burn these rags you wore 'ere," the matron declared, holding my blue frock up and inspecting it with disgust on her face. She held my fringed scarf in her chubby fingers, eyeing the workmanship.

"No! You shall not! I will wear my own clothes when I leave after I examine the injured man," I replied, outraged.

"Not likely," she snorted. "Where'd ye git dis 'ere scarf?" She asked, stroking the fringe in admiration.

"My mother made that!" I said, trying to take it back out of her hand but without success.

She snorted again as she pushed me back out into the hall and a short distance towards a closed pair of French doors, opening them roughly, and with her big body she pushed me through them and into a parlour where two young girls were lounging on settees. They appeared to be heavily in the drink from the half empty bottles and glasses on the tables. The room was large and round with crimson walls and large polished statues of nude women in beguiling poses. The smell of sour wine filled the air, confirming what the story told by the tipped over bottles and empty glasses strewn about. Polished dark tables and chairs gleamed invitingly. As I entered the room, the girls didn't look towards the door, but continued singing a badly slurred, off-key song.

"Woe is we
Who must go on at the party
Without thee,
Oh, my darlin' Caden,
Who's so very heavily laden,
When will you come back from yer fishin'
And give me what I am a wishin'!"

With that they fell into fits of giggling and sniggering. The girls appeared to be younger than me, but only just, and were well endowed and barely dressed. One girl had curly brown hair to her waist and that was almost all that she wore on her upper body, save for a very low neckline, thin cream-colored shift. One of her enormous breasts was completely exposed and hanging out of the garment for all to admire. With a coy look on her face, she played with her nipple as if to shock me. I looked away, startled and embarrassed. She smiled and laughed, showing a full array of blackened teeth. The other girl had darker hair that was pinned up with loose tendrils about her shoulders. She had milky white skin and was thinner than the other girl but was also very suggestively dressed and was positioned on the sofa with her legs askew. *"Caden?"* I said to myself. *"It sounded like they just said the name 'Caden'."*

"Oh, the new girl be here," the thinner of the girls said, very slowly and provocatively. "Come sit here so I can have a nice look at ye." She patted the sofa between her legs, again trying to shock me.

"Yes, do join us," said the curly-haired girl, now fingering a curl suggestively. Their vapid expressions and pouty mouths told me that sitting here waiting for the men of the party was their livelihood.

"Please, I don't understand. I am here to examine a wounded man..." I stammered in confusion, looking about the room, trying to make sense of the situation.

"The master's got a party invitation for ye," the curly-haired girl said, putting both of her hands up into her hair, extending her chest forward and arching her back provocatively.

The slimmer girl guffawed with laughter at these antics and said, through her laughing fit, "Yeah. They all wounded, ain't they?" With this, both girls curled up into fits of loud laughter, tears welling up in their eyes. I stared at them in disbelief.

When they had collected themselves, the curly-haired girl said, "You was summoned to provide some new entertainment. The 'tangled up with them all night' kind, if you git my meanin.'"

"She's not quite as smart as she thinks, is she now?" the thinner girl said, smirking.

"Please, I don't want to attend any party. So, there is no injured man? I am here by mistake," I pleaded, my eyes darting from one girl to the other. "Did you say the name 'Caden'?"

"Maybe 'oi did an maybe 'oi didn't," the thin girl answered, looking away.

"You did! You've been with Caden?" My voice sounded hurt and cracked. *He lied to me and William knew it. That is why William brought it up that day at the surgery. That is what their tense words were about. All this time Cade has betrayed me.* I was sickened.

"No mistake, and ye can be sartin. You be right pretty. I seed why the master wanted ye right badly. They be here any minute. We can show you what we do to entertain 'em afore they git 'ere," the curly-haired girl suggested with a straight face and the two girls burst out in fits of laughter again. The thinner girl poured herself a heaping glass of wine.

"Who? Who will be here?" I asked, my mind on full alert. I was sweating now, and my voice was shaking. I did not want any part of this wickedness. I clasped my hands together, wringing them in frustration.

"The men of the party. The master and his party be here any minute. Back from their fishin. Ye fell for the bait, that's for sure. Like a dumb Codfish." The curly-haired girl yawned and stretched, obviously tired from her previous night's activities.

I ran over to the door, but it was locked from the outside, of course. Then I ran to the large windows, pushing against them with my full body weight, but they wouldn't open.

"It's not so bad," said the curly-haired girl. "Here, have some of this brandy. With enough of this, ye migh' even enjoy it." They both giggled again. Hopefully, it will be quick, and ye can go 'bout yourn business. If they let ye."

"Not likely if it's more than one, an' it usually is. That takes longer," the thinner one said, nodding her head as if an expert on the subject.

Horrified, I began to panic. My breath was fast and ragged. *How could I be so stupid to come up here? William warned me. I never should have come.* I was frightened by the waves, the reflection, and now these horrid women and their threats. Think, I told myself, urgently. My grandmother came to mind. I walked slowly over to the curly-haired girl and looked down at the brandy bottle.

"May I, then?" I asked, with a sigh of resignation. Thinking quickly on my feet was something I had had to learn growing up with an abusive father and brothers. I was desperate and willing to do anything to get out intact.

She stretched out her hand towards the bottle and I snatched her hand by the wrist. I wrenched her thin wrist behind her back, jumping behind her on the couch, tripping a bit on the long skirt I was wearing. I grabbed her around the throat with my other hand to the amazement of both girls. Then, with both my hands enclosed around her throat, I pressed her arteries with my fingers until she felt the effects. Dr. Moyle had explained these blood vessels to me and my memory served me well. Her hands clawed at mine, but to no avail. From my position above and behind her, I had better leverage and strength. Her legs kicked but she was no match for my strength, thankfully.

"Jesus, what the 'ell are ye doin?" she wheezed. The thinner girl looked on, stunned.

"I am a woman of the dark arts, and I will kill your friend here if you get any closer." I began to make strange, whispering noises that I had heard my grandmother make. The skies outside had darkened, and I used this to my advantage. The thinner girl was unable to tear her eyes away at the spectacle unfolding before her. I called up an ancient power in a spell-binding chant, still compressing the curly-haired girl's throat as she struggled and gagged. Her face turned completely white. As I continued, drawing up energy from my own terror, she became faint with fatigue and fear.

I adjusted the limp girl's neck into the crook of my elbow, holding her tightly. Imagining the fishing party appearing at any second, I could feel my fear completely take hold of me, mind, and body. I thrust my pointed index finger over the furniture and toward the many paned windows. Abruptly, a casement blew open clanking against the wall outside. Lightning flashed with a hideous *flash* and *crack*. The girls shrieked and began to tremble and wail, terrified of my strength and sorcery.

Unsure of what I had just done, whether by my own force or sheer coincidence, I made my next critical move. "I want you to call for the woman to open the door. Now!" I screamed. The girls flinched and the thinner girl jumped out of her seat and ran to the door.

"Mrs. Finch, better come quick! Come quick!" the thin girl yelped. "Mrs. Finch!" she yelled louder at the locked door.

I could hear the woman's footsteps as she lumbered up to the door, her keys clanking and scraping as she unlocked one of the doors and opened it, unknowingly. I had edged the curly-haired girl off the settee and over to the door. As it opened, I pushed the door open with one hand and knocked the matron partially away from the door with the limp girl's weight in the other arm.

"I will kill your party girl here if you do not let me out of that door, and then what will your master say about you?" I yelled to the shocked, stumbling matron.

"Wha?" She mouthed, disoriented, as if we had awoken her from a midday nap. Her hair was in a kerchief, and she wore a robe with a sash around her waist.

I took advantage of her grogginess and continued to thrust the half faint curly-haired girl over onto the matron's side, using all my body weight, causing her to topple over on her left. I squeezed past her and through the open door. I gathered up the borrowed skirts and ran down the corridor that I came through like my life depended on it.

I ran past the nude paintings. I heard nothing behind me. I doubted the heavy-set matron or the drunken party girls could catch me, but I was terrified of running directly into the returning men. Would they come in through the front gate if they were returning from fishing? Should I find another door? Would the women cut me off with another side door? Speed was the only thing I could use as a weapon. I decided, since it was the only option I truly knew, to run out the front door and out the gate as fast as I possibly could. But what if the gate was locked?

I ran through the corridors, staying on the carpets as much as possible to avoid making any noise. Thankfully, when I reached the front door, no one was about. I paused and listened for a brief second. I gripped the knob and pulled. The door was open! I opened it only enough for me to exit and ran out, not looking left or right. I felt the element of surprise was on my side. Besides, dark, billowing clouds were now overhead, and torrents of rain fell sideways, soaking me in an instant. Undaunted, I ran straight for the gate, completely out of breath but never wanting to escape anything so badly in my life. My legs pumped like furiously as I held up the long skirts. The black gates were open but I saw Tom out of the corner of my eye running through the rain for shelter on the path, and he yelled out, "Ey! Wait!"

My heart pounding with a mixture of desperation and fear, I ran through the gates and darted down the lane. I ducked through the hedges to one of the caves I knew below the lane but above the rows of houses down at the harbour. The hedge branches scratched me as the wind howled and ferociously tore at my hair and garments, as if it was trying to snatch me back into the clutches of the sinister castle. I darted into the cave, one of the many places I used to hide as a child, sometimes for games with Cade or Melly and sometimes out of fear of my father.

The jagged rocks of the cave's entrance, concealed amidst the rocky cliffs, beckoned to me like a childhood friend from another time. As I stepped into the cave, the air changed, filled with a dank, muddy smell that clung to me like a warm cloak. Inside the cave was a world untouched by the light of day. I knew from previous visits there that the walls were rough-hewn and craggy rocks, but all was black today. I remembered as a child wondering if pirates had stayed in this very cave and if they had stowed any treasure here.

In my respite from my tormentors, my mind immediately shifted to my family and friends. What was happening to William and the other seamen out in this storm? Surely the waters were extremely rough and treacherous. Were my mother and grandmother safely at home and out of harm's way? *Please God, let Mother and Grandmother be safe and protect*

William, even Caden and Father, those liars, and the rest of the brave seamen out on the bay today. Was the reflection an image of my mother's death? I must get back to mother immediately was my fervent wish.

I stayed close to the entrance of the cave and caught my breath hoping that no one would find me if they were looking. Tom had seen me. The wind had transformed into a raging beast, and I hoped its roaring and lashing would prevent anyone from following me. I waited and listened. I wanted to cry at the horrendous events of the day. My father. The castle and my apparent deception. Cade's betrayal. The ominous thrashing waves I had felt in the carriage that didn't exist. The reflection that told of a disaster, possibly to mother or to someone. Huddled in the cave, I tried to calm myself. I tried to regain some of my inner strength. I rocked back and forth with my arms around my knees to warm myself.

Alone in the dimly lit cave, I was able to single out my thoughts. Isolated there as I was, only my inner thoughts and feelings existed. No other interference from the outside world conflicted with the comfort of my familiar hideout. With this, my inner connection to the waves and storm grew exceptionally loudly within me. That peculiar feeling that had begun in the carriage earlier now began to grow and become clearer. Something was happening out in the sea on an enormous scale. Something on a scale so terrible that it would become legend. And it was calling me.

Chapter Thirteen

A LEGEND IN THE MAKING

PORT QUIN, CORNWALL, U.K.

AUGUST 7, 1841

I could barely see through the deluge of rain as I ran down the slope and toward home, slipping and falling several times on my knees and backside. No one was about and no one was yelling the maritime call for help, "Haul! Haul! Haul!" I ran through the empty streets and finally reached our cottage and flung open the door.

"Effy! Where ye been, child? We been beside ourselves and worrit!" my mother said, wrapping her arms around me, cheeks tearstained.

"Oh Mother! I was at Doyden Castle, and the most terrible thing happened, but I am alright now. Gran, I'm so glad you are here and safe!" I ran over to the interior corner chair where Grandmother sat knitting, her long needles paused at the sight of me.

"Effy, my child. What are ye wearin'? Soaked to the skin. Take off those wet clothes." She pointed a bony finger at me in admonishment.

"No time to explain now. Gran," I said, kneeling to speak with her, the fire spitting from rain coming down the chimney. "Gran, something terrible is happening with the sea. Do you feel it too?" I clasped her hand and studied her face.

"Yes, child. Lambs to the slaughter," she whispered.

"Do you mean the lamb, Moses? My lamb that William found?" I asked confused.

"No. The sea. Lambs to the slaughter!" she said loudly. Tears started rolling down her cheeks.

Mother came to her side. "She is tired and the storm has upset her. She has been like this since yesterday. I brought her here thinking I could soothe her, but she be in a fit. Let me make ye some mint tea, Mum." Mother said to her as she stroked her hand.

I sat back on my heels, stunned. The wind shook the thatched roof and rattled the windows mercilessly. *Lambs to the slaughter*, I repeated to myself. Then it hit me. The visions of the watery graves of Father and Caden at the church. The sounds of the crashing waves. The storm. The reflection of me in Gran's lap with the Bible.

I turned sharply to my mother and said with my eyes stinging with tears, "The seamen are in grave danger! I must do something. A lifeboat!" I cried out.

"The ships went out to sea hours ago, Effy. They be miles out in the sea now. What can be done in this storm? Ye would never reach 'em. I forbid ye any boat out in dem waters now. No one be here to help ye with any lifeboat. Promise me." She grabbed my arms to restrain me. Her voice pleaded with me, knowing how headstrong I was.

"I must at least try. Maybe someone is down at the quay. Maybe someone is struggling in the water off Kellan Head. I must go." I was still wearing the soaked silk skirt and bodice from the castle. I quickly put on a woollen cloak that was hanging next to the door. "You prepare food and bandages here and I will help you when I get back." I hugged her and breathed in her smell as if for the last time. I left her whimpering in my wake as I tore through the front door. All I could think of was saving someone's loved one. Anyone. *Why didn't I think of this before? Why didn't I try to convince the seamen to take precautions before they left?*

The rain outside was deafening and blinding as I made my way down the lane to the quay, as if I was underwater. The gale was so loud it burned through my ears. I could barely see the open berths and the harbour before me. I called out, but the wind and the rain doused my words as if I had never spoken them. All I could see all around me was grey as the sharp needles of rain bit into my skin. I pulled the hood of my cloak around my face tightly as flying objects—branches, leaves, fishing tackle, anything loose and lying about—pummeled me and anything in their path with murderous force. I slipped and fell on the quay and felt shooting pains on my right hip and elbow.

Since the quay appeared empty, my only recourse was to search the shoreline directly on foot. I looked around for anything floatable that I could toss out into the water to survivors. I found a few pieces of wood and two cork buoys. I held them under one arm, and I used my other arm to pull myself through the storm. I cut over to the path, now too muddy to use, and hiked as best as I could up the grass, to Kellan Head. Fighting the wind and the mud exhausted me and I stopped several times, shivering against a rock. I would stop on my way back to check on Anne Carlyon. But I had to at least see if anyone was in the water…

What I saw could barely be believed. The storm, raging with an unparalleled fury, had transformed the normally fairly tranquil waters into a heaving, churning nightmare. The waves, monstrous in height, rose like towering mountains, crashing against one another with a deafening roar that reverberated through my very core. Never could I have imagined anything so frightening to behold. Each black mountainous wave was topped with a white threatening crest that loomed so high in the sky that I felt like a tiny helpless moth below it. The surge had risen so high as to be close to the top of the Head, threatening to overwhelm it. Our usually benevolent sea had become evil, no longer our gentle companion but a relentless adversary intent on consuming and destroying all in its path. I could not see any of the fishing fleet but could only imagine the struggles of every vessel fighting for its life in these demonic waters, their lives hanging in the balance as they fought against this merciless onslaught of pounding tonnage of almost supernatural water.

Overhead, the clouds and wind were in league with their wicked water ally, doing their part to add to the chaos. They were all three warring titans, swirling, twisting, and gnawing, their colours and edges indistinguishable from each other. As all three were of the same shades, I found it difficult to see where one began and the other left off. I felt suffocated by their violence.

My soul was intertwined with the very essence of the sea-men of Port Quin, and it bled with a profound ache for their suffering. Through the relentless downpour, I struggled to get sight of the fleet, or what had once been the fleet, or even any survivors, but the rain streamed into my eyes, making sight impossible. My heart was in a knot of helplessness and despair. Each gust of wind and every thunderous crash of waves was a witness to the desperation that I had to find survivors. I could hear the cries of the seafarers, either in my own mind or carried by the wind, I could not tell. They reached me in ghostly desperation.

"Cade, over here! Toss me that board!" I faintly heard a voice say. *Was that William? Oh my God, was that William's voice? Please save William, dear Lord!*" I sank to my knees next to a large boulder, partially sheltered from the howling wind. I prayed fervently, with all my might, that William might be saved, although I had no right. "*Please Mary and Jesus, save William that he might continue to do right in the world. That his light will continue to shine from you to us here. Oh please!*" I briefly saw William in my mind, his covered arms waving over his head, planks and objects of debris crashing into him, water splashing his face, his shoulder bobbing up and down barely above water but visible. Then the image was gone.

Within those moments, I felt my spirit had become entangled with the storm's fury and the unyielding power of destiny of life and loss. I was tied to the seamen's plight and their thoughts and cries echoed in my mind. I saw the scene of boats completely submerged again and again, each by a single mammoth wave, the crews and boats lost under the wave as if they never existed. Some of the boats rode to the top of the mountainous crests only to fall on their backs into the troughs, crushed by the onslaught of water. I saw seamen slide helplessly off their decks and into the cold water. I vomited in the grass at seeing these images. I had never seen anything so brutal. Cold to the bone, I stood. I tossed the useless lifesaving things I had taken into the sea, numbed inside and out with pain, and stumbled to the Carlyon house. I realised now that I had more than passing premonitions within me. I had some kind of sight.

"Effy." My father's voice came to me in the wind. His voice sounded raspy and choked. I shook my head and covered my ears with my hands. "Effy!" I heard him moaning. Beware the killer! Beware as he will strike again! Murderer!" I looked up and thought I saw an image of him in the mist but the rain was in my eyes. In that instant I realized my father must have perished out at sea. I shuddered and my insides clenched. I knew I had not merely imagined what I had just heard and seen. I blinked hard and looked around but the horrid, frightening image and sound were gone.

Chapter Fourteen

THE PAYMASTER'S BOX

PORT QUIN, CORNWALL, U.K.

AUGUST 7, 1841

I needed and wanted to be at home, but I could barely walk another step. I was even more emotionally exhausted than physically after what I had seen and heard. I saw Anne Carlyon standing on the path outside her house. She clutched at her hooded cape as the wind tried to whip it off her head. She called out to me, "Did you see any of the fleet?" William's mother reached out to me with her free hand.

"I saw some boats. That is, I am not sure. It was difficult to see very far." I stammered, afraid to tell her that I saw the fleet but not sure if it was in my mind or if I actually saw the boats themselves. She grabbed hold of my arm and together we braced against the wind and back into the quiet safety of her house. My ears rang from the strong wind beating against them. I slumped down in a kitchen chair and laid my head down on the table, exhausted.

"Effy, child, you are frozen and exhausted. Let me get you a blanket and a hot cup of tea. Some ham and bread as well." She ran over to the cupboard to fetch the food first and set it down on a ceramic plate before me and I was more than grateful. The tea kettle was already hot on the fire. She poured me a steaming cup of tea. I wondered at the mist of vapour from the kettle and how such a tiny wisp could turn into the ominous masses outside. Wrapped in the woollen blanket, I ate hungrily. The food barely touched my tongue, and I didn't feel it in my stomach, I was so empty.

Anne watched me eat, looking like the stoic seaman's wife that she was. She had been through storms before, when Charles had been out to sea. She had waited with terrible anxiety like this many times in her life. To talk about it seemed useless to her, was my supposition. I wanted to tell her that I heard William's words on the wind, but how would I explain it?

"I have something very strange to tell you. I can scarcely believe it myself at times. Please don't tell this to anyone else." I glanced at her, somewhat anxiously. "You see, my grandmother and I can hear and see things that others don't. A kind of dark art, I would call it."

"Yes, I had heard that about your grandmother. From the women in the village. That is rather strange, but I believe you," she nodded, solemnly. "And I will not mention it to anyone, ever, unless you allow it."

"I believe William is alive or was a few minutes ago." I pressed ahead, having decided to tell her. "I heard his voice in the wind. These premonitions that I have seem to come true.

I don't know if William knows this about me. I am not sure quite how to explain it other than I pray that it is true this time as well."

"What exactly did you hear?" she asked, trying to tamp down her excitement.

"I heard William say to Cade, 'Pass me that board,'" as if William was asking Cade for help to survive in the water."

"Do you think Cade was going to say 'yes'? That is, what was the tone of William's voice? Was it angry or were they seeming to work together?" She asked, in concentration.

"I'm not sure. I believe the tone was urgent but not angry. Why do you ask? That is, I am wondering if you know anything about a fight between them last night or this morning?"

"Yes, I saw them fighting last night. Yelling and pushing each other. Then Cade became furious and left. That is all I saw," she said, relaying the facts.

"If that is all you saw, then I am concerned. Cade came into the surgery with a bad knife wound on his thigh, about two inches long, but not terribly deep. Bleeding heavily. He told Dr. Moyle and I that William had done it during a fight this morning." I looked at her closely to gauge her reaction.

She paused, thinking of the facts. "William had gone to the quay early this morning to make ready for the day. When he left here, he had none of his fishing tools with him. That is, no knives. He left them all on the boat the night before. I doubt very much that he had any knife on him last night or this morning. I had sewn pieces of cork into the collar and vest of a coat that I insisted he take and wear. That was all he had that I saw. I pray to God he was wearing that coat." She sighed and laid her arms calmly on the table.

We sat looking at each other for a moment. "Dr. Moyle suggested that the angle of Cade's wound appeared that it could be self-inflicted," I stated.

"What do you think?" She asked, her large eyes passing no judgment.

"I am not sure what Cade is capable of anymore," I simply replied. "Why would he do such a thing? Cut himself?" I shook my head in sad disbelief.

"Love, or what he thinks is love, can do strange things to anyone. He apparently cut himself to get your attention," she said, softly, her eyes peering into mine.

"But that is deranged! And sad! Terrifying even!"

"Yes, it shows something of his inner self; his inner turmoil, I am afraid," she said without hesitation. "I pray to heaven they return, in any form."

"Yes, I just want them back as well." We shared aching hearts, the two of us. We sat there, deep in thought, listening to the wind howl in wounded misery.

"Thank you for giving me that shred of hope that William may still be alive," she said, after a pause, with a faint smile. "That William and Cade may still be alive." She reached out to take hold of my hand. I happily accepted its warmth. She was a strong, intelligent, fair, and kind woman and I was happy to have her in my life, even in a small way.

"I must get home now, or my mother will be sick with worry," I said, feebly pushing back my chair.

"Before you go, I must tell you that I was able to open the paymaster's chest," she said in a serious tone. "I opened it. I keep it in a cupboard in the workshop. Come. You must see what it contains," she urged.

"Shouldn't we wait for William...I mean. We should wait a bit longer to see if he returns." My voice trailed off and my eyes brimmed with tears. She leaned over in her chair and put her arms around my back and said, "We two will have to face the world with or without him, so we might as well start now. No sense in waiting. Come."

I nodded at her wise words and her sense of urgency, my energy returning somewhat. As we ventured outside, we battled the wind, which seemed to be subsiding. William's mother unlocked the door, pushing it open with her shoulder. She took me to a side room with a large cupboard. She asked me to turn around and close my eyes while she searched for a key to unlock it.

"To protect you, Effy, in case someone was to try to use the key against you, you understand," she warned.

"Oh, certainly. I understand," I replied quickly. The key looked like ancient brass with three coiled loops on top. She quickly opened the cupboard door, which swung open with a *creak.*

"Again, Effy, if you would turn your head, please," she asked.

"Of course," I nodded. I decided to walk out of the room and take a seat at the main work bench and wait for her to bring the box to me, which she promptly did, but not before closing the cupboard and storing the key, as I heard the safe creak again and close shut. *Even though I know she is not a pirate's wife, she certainly has a deliberate pirate booty secrecy about her,* I thought to myself. She came over to the bench and quickly sat down next to me. She set the black box down in front of me and I could see the lid was partially open.

"How did you get it open?" I asked.

"Never mind that now. Open it!" she quietly exclaimed.

I opened the box as instructed with no expectations at all. What I saw was pure magic and I felt myself gasp with shock. All the shiny, sparkling colours of the rainbow glistened before us and I hesitated to touch its enchantment. I looked up at Anne and she beckoned me with her eyes and face to touch it and make it real to the touch and the eyes. Within the confines of the box lay a collection of delicate and ancient-looking bejeweled broaches and pendants full of tiny purple and light green stones on silver and gold. The gems' colours burst forth, casting ethereal hues upon the dimly lit room. They shimmered like captured drops of a rainbow. Each stone was intricately set, each piece a testament to opulence and craftmanship worthy of a king. My eyes widened, as I knew that these jewels held unimaginable value.

"An incredibly valuable find, Effy," Anne whispered as she picked up one of the bejeweled brooches, shaped like a rounded, flattened fish. "These purple stones are amethysts. And these beautiful green ones are emeralds. Very possibly crafted over a century ago. I am astounded that you found this."

"How someone could set these tiny stones with such accuracy!" I sighed with awe.

"These tiny stones are actually quite large," Anne smiled.

The pieces whispered to me of a brighter future for William and the Carlyon shipbuilding venture. As I looked at each of the pieces, and there must have been twenty or more in the box, one stood out in particular. I picked it up and gasped in awe. I held up a cross with yellow stones, each about the size of my thumbnail and set in an intricate patterned gold Anne said was called "filagree." Between each stone was a small gold ball separating the stones from the gold setting. The gold filagree cross was the most beautiful piece in the box, partly because of its biblical nature, but also because of its colour and weight. The cross was deceivingly heavier than it looked.

"What type of stones are these? They are like the sun!" I exclaimed, amazed.

"I'm not entirely sure, but given the nature of the other stones, they could be yellow diamonds. If they are, this would be the most valuable piece in the box. This piece was contained in a small leather pouch, which was wet and decayed when I opened it. I cleaned it off and found the cross in perfect condition. I am guessing since it was in the pouch that someone wanted to take special care with this piece," Anne explained.

The yellow stones glistened in the pale light and gave me such a sense of hope that I pressed the cross to my chest. Immediately, I began to see scenes in my mind of William and his family prospering. Happily working outdoors on a ship. Another was an image of Anne with a small boy, laughing during a meal. A man, his father Charles, with a group of men looking at a large scroll of paper, a design, perhaps. A large white house, very pleasant looking on a body of water, small children dressed in white playing on a beach with starfish…

I pulled the gold cross from my chest and looked at it straight on. "Effy, what is it? Are you having a vision?" Anne asked, touching my arm and looking into my face.

"Yes, of sorts. I mean, I'm not sure. But it was happy. Nothing to be worried about." I placed the gold cross gently back into the box. My heart swelled with hope. I envisioned the ships that could now be built, grand vessels that would navigate uncharted waters and forge new paths across vast expanses of the blue oceans and reach new markets, opening channels for trade.

But there was more to these jeweled wonders than mere material wealth. As the winds continued to buffet the trees outside, my gaze stayed fast on each intricate piece. glimmering individually and as a mass, and my mind wandered to the poor fisher folk in town who could never hope to feed or clothe themselves. Was it right to take such treasure for oneself? The wealth in this box could be the key to feeding the poor or certainly opening a hospital, a sanctuary for the sick and wounded. Provide materials to build homes. Comfort. Safety. Certainly, it would be right to bring solace to those in need. Would it be right to leave the poor of Port Quin behind?

I put the lid back over the box and pushed it toward her. "I could never enjoy this without William. He was the one who found it in the first place," I said, near sobbing. My throat felt swollen with a huge lump in it and I couldn't say another word.

"Hush now, child. He said if anything happened, you were to keep this. I will return it to the cupboard. We won't speak of this to anyone now. Let's focus on getting through this storm and what we must bear." We faced each other and locked our forearms. I nodded. Totally trusting her judgment and honour, I turned my back as she returned the jewels and the box, concealed once again.

As she was locking the workshop door, a thought occurred to Anne. "Effy, forgive me for asking this but was William wearing the coat I made for him that was filled with the cork?

That is, in your vision, was he wearing a coat?"

I closed my eyes and tried to recollect what I had heard and seen in my mind. Water rolling up and down. Debris floating. William's arms over his head. And yes, a collar. "I saw his arm up over his head and a collar up around his neck. It was dark brown. What colour was the coat you sent with William?" I asked, fearing her answer but hoping William was in fact wearing her life-saving device.

"Brown." She replied, clasping my hand. "It was brown."

As I walked home, the skies were calmer, and the wind had died down. Early evening had fallen. I knew that the weight of many choices rested heavily upon me now. The fate of William's ship building venture—with or without him. The realization that the evil of greed, something I had never known in my entire life, could and would creep into my life now at any moment. The realization that I suddenly could fulfill my dreams of learning to heal and to provide healing was unreal and I felt like I was in a dream, floating on air but at the same time devastated that I had crushing news about the fleet. So many fates ran like currents in and from that paymaster's box and I because I saw a shimmering light, would be the one to navigate them like a ship's captain.

Upon finally returning home, I burst through the front door and fell into my mother's arms, out of breath, shivering. "What has happened? What did ye see?" She asked, anxiously, as she had been waiting for the nearly four hours I had been gone.

"I went to the quay and saw no one. I made it up to Kellan Head, and again, saw no one. The waves were monstrously big. Father did not survive. His voice came to me in the wind,

Mother, and in a calm tone. With no anger." She went to a chair and slowly sat down.

"Then clearly he must have passed." She clasped her hands together and began to pray.

Gran sat by the large front window so the last light would shine on the large Bible she had open. Through it, I could see how the waves snarled and bit at the rocky shore. "Christ is at the helm of every boat," she said, reminding me as she read passages, stoking my straggling hair with her wrinkled hand, that God is the greatest source of comfort of all. I went over to her and laid my head in one arm in her lap, my knees buckled up underneath me, and in complete despair, sobbed pent up tears over all the lost men, over William especially, still wearing the light pink bodice, and crumpled white skirt and petticoats given to me by the matron of the Castle. Exhausted, my arm rested on her strong body, my limp hand hovered over the Bible we all revered.

I realized I was living the reflection I had seen that day on the way to Doyden Castle. Now I knew what the reflection was trying to tell me. But how could I have known then? *Waves that I heard and grief that I saw should have been enough to put together what happened*, I told myself. *I should have warned them. But they were already gone.* I felt as if I was living in a kind of nightmare.

Behind Grandmother, an altar-like offering had been set up in hopes of the seafarers' return. Cheese, bread, and mackerel sat uneaten on the table draped with our plain white tablecloth. Candles burned down through the night with no one to appreciate their light. The lamp at the window was almost completely burned out and behind it our seaweed hung full of moisture, telling the story we already knew, that rain was in the air. We stayed there all night, praying and waiting for someone to come home. We stayed there until dawn, helpless and hopeless.

FRANK BRAMLEY'S COTTAGE, NEWLYN, CORNWALL, SITE OF PAINTING
A HOPELESS DAWN (1880)

EXCERPT FROM *A SUMMARY OF MEMOIRS OF THE PARISH OF ST. ENDELLION PRIOR TO THE YEAR 1834*

Port Quin

CASTLE ROCK, A FAVORITE FISHING SPOT,
ILLUSTRATED BY JOHN WATTS TREVAN, 1834

JOHN HAWKIN'S MILL AT PORT QUIN,
ILLUSTRATED BY JOHN WATTS TREVAN, 1834

ABRAHAM BASTARD PREACHING IN PORT ISAAC,
ILLUSTRATED BY JOHN WATTS TREVAN, 1834

The *Charles Tucker*, 1835,
Imagined as Captain Phillip's Schooner

The schooner CHARLES TUCKER, owned by William Henry Williams of Newquay, and the Cardiff pilot cutter POLLY, drying sails in Clovelly.   *Royal Institution of Cornwall*

Chapter Fifteen

SEA KELP RIBBONS

PORT QUIN, CORNWALL, U.K.

AUGUST 8, 1841

Dawn broke. The candles had burned down completely. The first tendrils of the sun pierced through the dark veil of the night and the blanket of clouds, casting a pale glow upon the washed-out streets of Port Quin. Mother and I joined the weary-faced women who opened their doors and gathered at the quay, bringing blankets and food. Our anxious and exhausted eyes, filled with dread, scanned the harbour first and then the horizon, searching for signs of the returning fleet and our husbands, fathers, sons, and neighbors.

And then, in the distance, the silhouettes of a handful of boats emerged, first one, then two more, and then a total of five. We all stood at the quayside, cheering, and expected then to see many more, but there were only five. Five out of thirty were all that came back. The air became thick with apprehension as the weight of our collective hopes and fears, with a heavy amount of guilt, as we all hoped for our own men over everyone else's, if the truth be told.

The five remaining ships struggled in, each at their own slow pace, battling with what as left of their sails and rigging from the hellish night. Some of the women gasped, their knees hitting the ground as they realized that a boat was "theirs" or not theirs. Some cried prayers of gratitude while many others went back to their homes to begin what would be their long grief, their footsteps echoing in an eerie unison on Quay Street.

For five boats carried back thirteen sailors but left thirty-two at the bottom of the sea. I had visions of the lost fishermen as I stood at the quay. All at once, my mind began to fill with images of dark green sea kelp beds under the waves. Long lengths of green sea kelp ribbons spun in the water, as if reaching for the lifeless seamen, whose hair and arms floated, slowly drifting down to the sandy bottom. A few last remaining bubbles popped out of some of their mouths and clothes. Curious yellow fish darted in and out of old Mr. Tambling's white hair. A peaceful scene after all the fear he had faced. I was glad of that much at least. Not far from him, I saw Mr. Lacombe, my neighbor, who had a peculiar superstition about seeing rabbits while onboard a ship, along with members of his crew. I also saw Mr. Hicks, whom folks said could whistle up the wind when there was none, and Mr. Tremaine, whom William and I had seen happily playing his fife, both of whom had been at the church recently. Their bodies were weighed down with heavy rope, perhaps used to keep them tied to their ships and their faces had a blue tinge. My only consolation for them was that they were now at peace with their Maker. But these visions were not something I could explain or convey to wives and mothers sick with grief and fear of their own unknown futures.

The mammoth storm had created a hopeless dawn for many that morning. Many wives with no husbands. Many children woke up that day with no father. Mothers with no son. Without enough men in the village, the women would teeter precariously on the edge of starvation and poverty. As the morning became afternoon, this realization was piercing the hearts and minds of scores of families.

Dr. Moyle and I stood ready at the quay with alcohol and bandages to tend to the wounded. The crowd was hushed as each ship approached, worn, and battered, with the seamen looking even worse. Their expressions were gaunt and etched with the unmistakable signs of a harrowing, grisly ordeal. They had the look in their eyes of seeing the untimely deaths of family and friends and being helpless to do anything about it. Worn and beaten, they disembarked from what remained of their vessels.

Cade, miraculously among the survivors, came back on the *Theodor* rather than with his own crew. He stumbled onto the quay; black bruises exposed where his clothes had been torn away. He had battled the monstrous forces of nature and lived to tell the tale. My heart was gripped with relief and anguish, and it propelled me forward until I stood before him, my eyes filled with tears of gratitude despite his wicked betrayal and lies. Yet, I also felt a mix of confusion over what I thought I heard during the storm. Had Cade helped William as William had begged? I yearned to know the answer to this question and of course, where William was.

The women surrounded the survivors, embracing their loved ones in a mix of joy and sorrow woven in their tight embraces. Their relief was tinged with the realization of the immense toll the sea had exacted upon their men for only doing their daily work. The stories spilled forth, mingling with sobs and curses, the mountainous waves that swallowed entire boats and crew, the relentless fury of the storm, the bravery of those who fought tooth and nail against the raging tempest. Some of the tones were hushed and some were animated. But through the commotion, I distinctly heard several men mention bravery. Brave men, like William Carlyon, who had attempted to save other men.

But William was not among those on the quay. I searched around repeatedly, looking for his tall head among the small crowd, but he was not among them. My whole body shrank in desolation. My heart ached for William and the others who did not return, but most especially for my precious William. I saw Mr. Trelights, Mr. Jenkin, and the ragged others. Mr. Collins, whose five young children certainly needed their father, was there. I felt profound sadness for those who had fallen. At that moment, I was acutely aware of the fragility of life.

With complete numbness, I tended to the injured men, some with broken bones, lost teeth, and battered spirits. Dr. Moyle and I bandaged them at the quayside and then they were carried away to seek solace and healing. Dr. Moyle turned to Cade.

"Are you feeling any pain other than these bruised areas that I see here?" Dr. Moyle asked, pointing to Cade's forearms. He felt Cade's arms and then his middle body. Satisfied with his examination there, Dr. Moyle's hands gingerly felt Cade's head. "Were you struck in the head at all?" He asked Cade.

"Struck in the head?" Cade echoed, laughing and sniggering. "No, not me. I tumbled in the water, but nothing is broken," he replied.

"And what about that knife wound. Can I examine that?" Dr. Moyle asked, pointing to Cade's thigh.

"It's fine." Cade snapped, and with that he accepted a blanket from a neighbor.

Cade clung to me, so grateful to be alive. "Effy, your father. He didn't make it. I am so sorry to have to tell you."

"I know. I too am sorry for him," I said earnestly. "That was no way for anyone to pass."

"Many friends also perished. A terrible sight. I almost died several times myself. I almost drowned so many times. Waves engulfed me, full on sucked me under," he said, half crying. "I am so grateful to see you," he said, kissing my cheek and starting to laugh.

"Cade, what about William? What happened to him? Did you see him?" I couldn't help but ask Cade about William and the words I had heard William speak that came to me over the wind. I was so torn up inside I had to ask him, regardless of how untimely it may have seemed.

"I saw the *Mary* go down," Cade recollected. "Then I saw the *Hope* rock sideways, and it was sideswiped by a giant wave. I saw the crew tossed into the water. But I never saw William. I assume he was washed away with the crew." Cade rubbed his dirty hands across his face. Then he laughed for no apparent reason, his teeth showing through the salty grime, as handsome as ever.

"You never spoke to William out in the water?" I asked.

"No, Effy. I never did. Why do you ask? What is it about William? Why so many questions about William?" Cade asked, his hands out to his sides palms up, laughing loudly as if I had just told him a hilarious story at the inn.

Not wanting to push Cade's fragile mental state into a collapse after the anguish he had just been through, I simply said, "His mother wants to know, Cade. Now, it's time for you to return home to your mother. And your sisters. I am sure they are sick with worry."

"Yes. They will be relieved to see me. Although I dread having to tell them about all this. But I will ask to see you after I sleep for a bit and I still have that question to ask you, remember?" He said, wagging his index finger at me with a smile and laughing giddily. I patted his back, and several neighbors came over to help him return up Quay Street towards the church to return home.

Dr. Moyle glanced over at me, warily. "Best to leave him to recover for a while. His mental state being what it is, I am afraid he needs time to rest after what he has been through."

I dried my hands on a towel and put several unused bandages back in my basket to return to the surgery. The fickle sun shone brilliantly now as if the worst storm anyone had ever known had not just devastated our livelihood and killed scores of our men. The sun wasn't the only fickle thing that burned my mind and heart. *'Never saw William.' I know that's a lie. I know I heard William ask Cade for help, for a board to float with. Cade knows something. What is he hiding? And I have the most peculiar feeling that William is still alive. Where is he?*

Dr. Moyle turned to me and asked, urgently, "Effy, did you take my bottle of elixir of morphine? It was here in my case and now it's gone."

"No, Dr. Moyle, I haven't seen it." We looked at each other, concerned, and he scavenged through his bag. The bottle was nowhere to be found.

"Someone must have taken it," Dr. Moyle said under his breath, grasping the sides of his bag as he searched again, alarmed, and shaken.

Chapter Sixteen

LOST ON LAND AND AT SEA

PORT QUIN, CORNWALL, U.K.

AUGUST 10, 1841

In the first few days following the storm, I barely left the quay. Anne watched the headland. We waited for news from the shoreline searches of the wreckage. I asked every passerby about news of William. Each day stretched out like an eternity hoping for news of just one more survivor that would surely come to shore. Anne and I sent messages to Port Isaac, Newquay, and Padstow with information about William and whom to contact if someone fitting his description was found. At least twice a day I went to the Turbot Inn to ask Melly and her father if they had any news from the men searching the shoreline for wreckage and bodies that washed up. No one did.

Parson Hockings was overwhelmed with his duties consoling grieving families and determining when to and how to conduct proper services for the men lost at sea. Due to the number of deceased involved, he decided the most fitting and reasonable approach was to have two services, one in the morning and one in the evening, each commemorating each man by name and the parishioners could attend one or both, although there would be standing room only for many. By having two services, he hoped to accommodate everyone who wished to attend at St. Minver. Mother and I decided to attend both services.

The services were terribly difficult to get through, of course. Prior to the first service, Mother and I had come early to get properly seated. As we were walking into the church, I shivered, dreading the service. Dr. Moyle approached me and I was glad to have a few seconds more to avoid the impending agony.

"Effy, a word please." I nodded to Mother and she continued walking into the church. Dr. Moyle leaned toward my ear and said in a low voice, "I found Cornelia." I turned to him with a surprised glance. With all that had happened with the storm, I had forgotten about the missing girl, my father's romance with her, and her poor father, the grain miller, Mr. Hawkins, who had been searching for her high and low. He nodded, anticipating my next questions. "She was found badly beaten in a room at a questionable pub just outside of Padstow. She won't say who it was that did it but that he threatened her mother if she didn't come along quietly. Given her description of the man, a certain man who matches that description who also has a recent illness of the mind, and who has also had whereabouts unknown…" He paused and gave me a hard, knowing stare.

"No!" I said, reading his face. "Not Cade!"

"I'd say it was likely. But again, she won't say who it was." And with that, Dr. Moyle strode off and entered the church, leaving standing there speechless at the entrance.

The service was about to begin. I had asked Anne Carlyon to join us, which she agreed to, even though she and I both still waited for William to return. We exchanged sideways, knowing glances inside the church, feeling awkward that William's name would be read aloud during the service. Her eyes had dark circles under them and she looked very weary as if she hadn't slept in days. We both still held on to hopes that somehow his brown cork coat enabled him to survive. A dim hope, but hope, nonetheless.

I was glad that I had no further visions prior to entering the church of loved ones coming out of the nearby graves as I had that day after working at the surgery. I shuddered as I remembered that grotesque scene. Since Cade was alive, the vision had been apparently just that, a vision of some kind, and it had been incorrect at any rate, so I chose to ignore it as some deeply disturbed bad daydream.

Cade slid into the open seat next to me. He appeared well, cleanly shaven, and rested. He gave me a polite smile and began his prayers, his hands placed together. Some of his bravado seemed to have faded. I was horrified to be sitting next to Cornelia's possible abductor. I had no reason to doubt Dr. Moyle's words and the fact that Cade seemed to think he could slide back into a respectable life, especially here in the church, made my blood run cold. All I could do at that moment was sit there in disgust at his lies and desolation over the loss from the storm.

As I looked around at the pale and somber faces, I had no

doubt what was on everyone's minds now compared to the last time I was here and wondered what was on everyone's mind. Loss. Emptiness. Grief. And dread. I waited for Parson Hockings's Adam's apple to begin to dart up and down again as he began his sermon.

In the dimly lit sanctuary of the old church, for it was a cloudy day out matching our somber moods, the stone walls echoed our grief and despair. Parson Hockings stood tall; his grave countenance and his dark vestments both suited the sorrow of the day. The flickering candles cast tiny eerie shadows upon the timeworn walls which had seen many tragedies, but nothing like this one, I reckoned. The ancient stained glass, ordinarily bright and colourful, seemed muted and dulled as if it too was mourning, adding to the atmosphere of melancholy.

The church atmosphere told the story of death in many ways but for the smell. The smell inside those four walls was all too alive. The crowded pews reeked with body odor from the living in the sweltering summer heat. In addition, some of the living were feeling poorly, it seemed, from the gaseous smells that came from anxious stomachs. Many appeared to be suffering from poor eating and perhaps overindulging in ale or liquor to dull the pain and the rest of us suffered in close quarters. I had nothing with which to fan away the odours, so I put my chin to my chest where I had attached a large sprig of lavender to the top of my bodice for this very purpose.

The parson cleared his throat. His voice trembled a bit with a mixture of compassion for the magnitude of the loss and trepidation as he viewed the tearful assembly before him. His words, laden with the weight of the loss, were carefully chosen to offer solace and hope to us, the anguished souls that hung on his every word.

"My dear brethren," he began, his deep voice reverberating through the hallowed space, "we gather here today, burdened by a tragedy that has shattered our spirits and tested our faith. The tempestuous sea, that mistress that gives both life and death, has claimed the lives of our brave men, leaving our hearts heavy with grief."

He paused, allowing his words to soak into our burdened minds. His eyes scanned our tear-streaked faces, looking to see, I gathered, if he had made any connection, any glimmer of understanding amidst our numbness. With a softness that belied his own sorrow, he continued, "In these harrowing times, when the embrace of darkness threatens to overtake us, we must turn to the scriptures for advice, seeking solace and strength in the words of our Lord."

Parson Hockings reached for a worn leather-bound Bible, its pages frail looking and yellowed with age. As he opened it, a feeble whisper escaped its ancient bindings, as if the spirits of the past yearned to be heard once more. I heard a voice say, "You, dear loved ones, were all the seamen thought of as they went down. Carry on their legacy. Make all those that came before you proud by carrying on their faith and way of life."

Because I had felt I was at one with their minds during the horrors of the event, I knew this voice speaking to me now was the same messenger that had tried to forewarn me of the loss I had felt and heard earlier, before the storm, here in the church and that it now spoke the truth. That this was what the seamen wanted more than anything now that they were free from the storm at last. For us, their pride and joy, to move on with them in their hearts and make the choices that only we could make, following what they had taught us as best as they could. I was proud to have known them all and vowed to remember how they loved us through the daily grind of struggle that was our way of life. How I wished I could have understood the message and done something to protect all these innocent men! I felt a terrible sense of guilt at not heeding the messages about the storm. To think I might have prevented all of this. How I wished these suffering families could hear their message now as I could! That would give them some solace at least, I thought. I turned to glance at Mother, but I could tell she had no knowledge of the message from this ancient voice.

The Parson found his chosen passage, marked with trembling hands, and he began to read.

"Yea, thought we walk through the valley of the shadow of death, we shall fear no evil, for thou art with us, thy rod and they staff, they comfort us," he recited, his voice rising and falling with the rhythm of the words. The sacred verse reached through the pain to touch the hearts of those who listened, casting a thin ray of hope amidst the murky depths of their despair. I wondered if anyone felt the pride that I did.

Turning to gaze to the families who had suffered immeasurable loss, the parson's voice softened further, carrying a sympathetic tone that seemed to bridge the gap between the earthly realm that he stood on and the celestial beyond. "To you, dear souls, who have been left behind, burdened with the weight of carrying on with sorrow, I implore you to find solace in the belief that your loved ones have been called to a realm beyond the reach of earthly pain, suffering and worry." He paused, his eyes glimmering with unshed tears, his words heavy with his own sadness. "They have embarked upon a voyage to a serene haven, where the storms of life cannot battle them, in the embrace of our merciful God, they shall find eternal peace, their souls cradled by His loving hand."

The Parson's voice, both gentle and firm, permeated the chapel with a sense of unwavering hope and the strength we badly needed. "Let us draw strength from their courage, their unwavering service to us, their families, as we embark upon our own journey through the tempests of life. For it is in the face of such trials that our faith is tested, and it is through our faith that we shall find solace, peace, and the courage to do justice to their legacies."

As the final echoes of his words faded into the expanse of the ceiling of the church, a stillness settled over the congregation, and I grabbed Mother's hand. She clutched it in return and bent her head near to mine and said, "We will rise or fall together, you and I." Many in the church remained in the pews, deep in their own thoughts or prayers.

"Effy, could I please have a word outside?" Cade quietly asked. Mother nodded to my dread. I was hoping to avoid a direct conversation with Cade.

I was completely on my guard with Cade, knowing that he was likely hiding facts not only about himself and William, but about Cornelia now as well. I vowed to get to the bottom of whatever it was. Mr. and Mrs. Buller, the shoemaker, and his wife, had also stepped outside and stood only a short distance from us. Mrs. Buller carried their baby boy, James, in her arms wrapped in a light white blanket with pale blue embroidered flowers on it. Mr. Buller wiped his eyes with his handkerchief, sobbing. He glanced over at us, trying to control his grief.

"I keep thinking of all the boots I have in my shop for repair. Boots whose owners aren't coming back. What am I to do with these boots?" His shoulders shook as he sobbed uncontrollably and looked sadly away, shaking his head as his wife gently took his arm and they began the long walk back to Quay Street.

I turned to Cade. "Before you say anything, Cade, you should know that I am still waiting for William, and I intend to keep looking for him." I said emphatically.

Cade nodded, looking down at the grass in the churchyard. "I understand. You have strong feelings for him, and you are holding on to hope that he is still alive."

"Yes, exactly. As strange as this may sound, I heard him that day in the wind saying to you, 'hand me that board,' or something to that effect, as if he was asking for your help. Did you help him? Did you see him alive?" I pressed.

"I did. I did see him alive, right before he went under for the last time. There was no board, Effy. I saw him go under and not come up. I saw it with my own eyes. I didn't say so before because I thought it would be too cruel at the time. I believe he is gone. Sorry to say that when you still have hope, my darling," he said, softly.

I didn't know what to believe. He sounded so convincing. I stood there, trembling. "Nevertheless, I will still search for him," I said, defiantly.

"I see. Listen, I wanted to tell you that folks are making plans. Plans to move from Port Quin." I listened to him tell me what I suspected but didn't want to hear or discuss. "As you and your mother think about your own intentions, let me offer this. I can offer protection in a man's world. I am not without means and I can find work. I ask that you consider me in your plans as my offer of marriage still stands. Think of your mother, your grandmother."

I looked up at his face. He seemed very calm and rational. He looked at me with sincerity. His handsome face seemed only concerned for me and my welfare. After the sermon, I couldn't help wanting to be taken care of by someone capable and strong. My guilt weighed on me heavily. But if what Dr. Moyle said was true about him abducting Cornelia, I was staring into the face of a monster who wanted to be my guardian. I couldn't think of how to get rid of him fast enough. "I don't know, Cade. I am overwhelmed now and Mother and I have not discussed what we are going to do."

"I understand. Very well. As a token of my esteem and my commitment, please accept this gift then." He reached down for my hand and pressed a small leather bag with a rope string into it. "Please, open it."

"Cade. What is this?" I expanded the tiny purse and pulled out a lovely white pearl pendant surrounded by swirling silver mounting. The pendant was on a fine braided silver chain.

"Cade!" I exclaimed. "Where did you get such lavish piece?" I asked, astonished, knowing full well that he could never afford such a piece of jewelry.

"I won it in a card came," he responded, casually, shifting his weight from one leg to the other.

"A card game? Where?" I asked, incredulously, looking down at the lovely pearl.

"Oh, at the Turbot. A few weeks ago. I play there a lot. A fellow who came to a party at the castle had lost all his cash and all he had left was this. Said it was his wife's. Here, let me put it on you," he said.

"It is lovely, but I can't accept this. Such an expensive…"

"Please keep it for now. I would feel happy if you did," Cade said, smiling.

I looked at him, seething and before I could think I spat out, "Cade, you are a dirty liar. You were with the girls at the Doyden Castle. I know it."

"What? What girls?" He looked at me dumbly. "Who said that? Was it William?"

"No," I said slowly. "It was a curly haired girl and a thinner girl who said it themselves. Directly to me."

"Oh, them," Cade laughed. "I've seen them there when I was making deliveries. They have tried to lure me in but I have never agreed. I promise you, Effy, that is not true. I have never been with those foul trollops."

I wasn't expecting that response. "I…but they…" I stammered.

"Forget them," he said, dismissing them with a wave of his hand. "Remember, your mother and grandmother will need means of support. I can help. Think about it." His strong hands rested on my shoulders, and I felt their warmth ooze down through my body. My flesh sprang to life. I bit my tongue and stepped back, feeling trapped. I didn't want to take his gift and with the paymaster's box, I didn't need his gift. But I also didn't want to anger Cade given the frail state of his mind and his violent undercurrent with a knife, and who knew what else, which I knew lay just beneath that mild surface. *No more swooning over a handsome face, Effy. No more! This is your last warning.*

"Thank you for the gift, Cade." His chin lifted slightly, as if he had accomplished some score he had longed to settle. "But my family and I will try to make do on our own."

In the days after the five boats returned to Port Quin our lives were full of holes and empty spaces where people used to be. Our fish stores began to empty, even though there were far fewer mouths to feed. The fact was, the few boats remaining were not seaworthy, and many of the seamen were still recovering, so Port Quin had far fewer hands to catch the fish. Many of the widows decided to pack up their few belongings and move to Port Isaac, the next port to the north, as it was a bigger town and very close, only two miles up the coast. There, they hoped to find jobs weaving nets, cleaning and hauling fish, or whatever else they could do.

Our new circumstances were a frightening new reality for Mother, Grandmother, and me, however, we also felt comfort for the first time in our lives. After the church services that were held for those missing at sea, Gran, Mother, and I took our first full breaths as the weight of my father's frightening presence was lifted. We made our own rules about meals, what we wore, who we saw, what chores we did, and how we lived. I borrowed a book from Anne and tried to focus on it to curb my grief. I did feel sorrow for the loss of my father, however flawed he might have been. Mother felt the loss of her husband, the keen navigator of the sea and of life. And while we rarely spoke of him, when we did, we did so kindly, for he had been a strong provider, and would have protected us against anything.

One evening, Mother, Grandmother and I sat down to supper of rabbit stew, a blessing since our rabbit traps were still producing and our garden still plentiful. "Mother," I asked, "what should our plans be?" I thought back to Cade's questions earlier in the churchyard. "Other women are moving to Port Isaac where work is more plentiful. Perhaps we should consider that as well. I can't see my brothers moving back here to help us, can you?"

"No. They have their own life on the farm. Hard to say what we should do," Mother replied, thinking it over, staring down at her plate. I realized a move would be difficult for Mother, having lived here in Port Quin her entire life. "If we don't move soon, many of the jobs may be taken, but the looming and knitting jobs may still be open, as they have been."

"I will stay here. I plan to remain," Grandmother interjected, rather rudely, as usual steadfast in her wishes and opinions.

"That is well and fine, but how will we support you if we move to another port?" Mother asked, very calmly.

"Ye can visit, if ye like." Grandmother replied, cheekily. Mother and I smiled at her in response.

"Mother, I may be able to support us in another way, other than the weaving," I said, vaguely.

"If it has anything to do with Cade, I am wary of him, as ye know. Don't rush to him because of us," she said, pointing at herself and Grandmother.

"I was thinking of something else. Perhaps I will tell you more at another time." I wasn't sure if I should tell her about the treasure before discussing it with Anne or not. In my mind, I was considering taking a piece of the treasure to London to have it appraised and sold, just enough to hold us over until we figured out what to do...perhaps buy a house somewhere where all three of us could live...I was playing with the pendant that Cade had given me, twisting it about my fingers.

"What is that ye have around yer neck, child?" She asked.

"Cade gave me this as a gift...of friendship. I think it is quite valuable," I answered, hoping not to have to reply to any more questions about Cade's intentions with the gift.

"Hold it out, so that I can seed it better." Grandmother squinted her eyes. "Is that a pearl set in silver?"

"Why yes, it is," I said, growing a bit more concerned at her interest.

"Umhmm. As I thought," she grunted with certainty. "I seed one same like that."

"But how could that be, Mother? Ye must be mistaken," Mother said, softly.

"Not mistaken. My dear friend of thirty years, Emily Hathoway, had one exactly like that. Her husband gave it to her as a wedding gift. She died about a month ago from consumption if ye recall?" Grandmother resumed eating her stew, slurping loudly.

Chapter Seventeen

BELIEVE THE WIND

PORT QUIN, CORNWALL, U.K.

AUGUST 16, 1841

I sat on the white window ledge in our home, my chin in my hand, staring out at passersby in the dim morning light. The ledge felt hard and cold beneath me, but I barely noticed this discomfort. The relentless wind howled and tugged at everyone's hats, skirts, and bonnets. Black-headed gulls screeched and cawed as they circled overhead in their usual hunt for scraps by the quay and on the street. I took little notice of them.

I had barely slept again. Working all day before and late into the evening at the surgery with Dr. Moyle helping the wounded seamen had taken its toll on my ability to get any rest. Dr. Moyle was overwhelmed with patients that needed to be seen and asked for my assistance not only during the day but in the evening as well, which interfered with my search for William. Several of the seamen's wounds had become in-flamed and needed attention. Many of the men also had wounded minds from what they had seen and because they had survived while the others had not—evident from vacant gazes and stories of nightmares from their wives. But what bandages and salves could be used for wounds of the mind and soul? We didn't know. We had worked together silently and tirelessly without discussing William or Cade.

I sat on the ledge and thought. *Another night has passed. A bad sign for finding William.* My mouth was dry, and my body ached from the hard work at the surgery and from sitting still too long. I felt like a sculpture carved from a rock of hard anguish. Worry was etched deep into my bones, much less my skin. I wondered if I would ever see William again. I tried to summon the feeling I had had that William was still alive, but the feeling seemed to have faded. Because of that, instead of feeling the exuberance of youth and girlhood I once knew, now all that I felt was hopeless and joyless. As if I would never feel cheerful again.

Mother stopped her cleaning chores to take my limp hand. "I think Dr. Moyle be workin' ye too hard. Might be that he's taking advantage, Effy." She paused and stroked my back with her strong hand. "Your gaze is very distant and sorrowful these days. Some things are out of our control, Effy."

"Yes. I know." I responded lethargically, not looking at her.

"Your smile used to be so pretty and your laughter so gay. I used to live for one of your good belly laughs. Now your mouth is only sad and downturned. Yeu used to have buckets o' energy. Now ye seem to carry the weight of the world on your shoulders," she said, stroking my hair gently with her fingernails.

"I am but a painting of melancholy now, Mother. My whole being is only sorrow. Like the agony of the winds that can never stop, never find solace." A solitary tear rolled down my cheek.

She sat down next to me on the sill and cradled me in her arms. She rocked me back and forth like a small child who had lost its favorite toy. "All is not lost. Ye cannot escape the difficult days-yeu can only live through them. Time will come to your aid. Somehow, it will ease your pain. I know it," she soothed.

"Mother, I am disturbed by my visions and premonitions. I can't control when they come and I don't rightly know what they mean. They take possession of me and I am confounded. What can I do?" I asked her, pleading for an answer I knew she couldn't give.

"It were a time long ago when I too had some visions. Your Gran tried to teach me about them but they frightened me too much. I pushed them away and pulled in the Lord. Maybe I done wrong," she said with a weak smile. "Turn to your Gran for help. She is a wise one with visions."

Her warmth and strength were my light to guide me and cling to, always. "But now, let us busy our hands to calm our minds and strengthen our souls. Come now. Idle hands are the Devil's workshop. We have knitting and spinning to do." She lifted me by the arm and my soul followed.

We sat for several hours, knitting on which I did my best to focus my attention as I sat with my needles and yarn in hand, clicking the needles together and making long rows of neat stitches-not too tight and not too loose. Yet, I found myself losing track of whether I had placed my yarn over my needle or not. I had recurring thoughts of Henry, William's brother, running down from the Carlyon house to tell me something urgent. Images of Henry, running as fast as he could, yelling my name. I could feel my heart starting to pound. I tried again to concentrate on the work and shift my mind away from this image. *Why am I seeing this over and over?* Henry, with his light brown hair flying backwards, his arms pumping and his legs in full gallop. I had the most peculiar feeling coming over me—a powerful feeling of hope.

I stood up quickly and my knitting fell to the floor, my yarn ball rolling away in a dizzying whirl. I felt compelled to run to the door and fling it open.

"Effy?" My mother called after me, in a strangled voice.

"Let her go," I heard Grandmother say.

Henry *was* there, running down the coast path, waving his arms, his mouth open, yelling something. I ran out the door, leaving it open, no bonnet on, and ran toward him, my heart pounding in my chest.

"Effy, a ship," he panted and pointed back toward the headland. "A ship has anchored in the bay and a boat is rowing towards shore. Come quick!" Henry pulled at my sleeve, having not stopped moving, and we gathered up speed to a run down the slope and around the quay. In that instant, I knew that William was on the ship and was alive. My heart expanded to an enormous size filled with joy, and I felt as light as a bird, soaring as if I had wings.

The boat was in fact just pulling up to the quay and appeared to have two men rowing and three passengers aboard. I saw Anne waiting on the quay her arms waving around her body. Henry and I ran to greet the passengers as the rowers tied the mooring lines. Other people on the streets pointed at our commotion and came over to see what was happening. William stood up in the boat first, causing it to wobble and jumped on to the quay and into his mother's arms.

"Mother! Oh, Mother!" He cried, his large arms completely engulfing her body. He smiled, his head bent down to touch hers, and the boat passengers cheered. He had a large white bandage wrapped around his forehead and over the top of his head.

"My darling boy! You're alive! You're alive!" I heard her sob repeatedly in choked tears from under his embrace.

Without waiting my turn, I ran to them, and so did Henry, and wrapped my arms around them. William grasped the back of my head with his hand and pulled my face close to his and said, "Your face kept me going. I am here."

"William, thank God! You're alive!" I cried. Henry pressed in behind his mother and William encircled his back with his hand. Several men and more women joined us and cheered heartily. I didn't want to let go of William's body. To see him standing there in the flesh seemed merely like my imagination. I was breathless and speechless. To touch him and to feel his warmth, alive and well, was too good to be real. I blinked my eyes as it was difficult to see between the tears.

"He's home! William's come home!" The crowd and onlookers cheered and clapped. "To the Inn!" one of the men called. We all melted into one. The crowd insisted that William and his family be celebrated at the Turbot Inn, and he was only too happy to oblige. He was smiling ear to ear as everyone was touching not only his hands but his face, arms, and chest. Anne and I hugged and wept out of pure joy and disbelief in our good fortune. I asked a small boy to run to tell my mother and grandmother and ask them to join us at the inn for this special occasion. Everyone wanted to hug and kiss William and were so thankful that another one of Port Quin's men had made it home.

As our happy mob pushed into the Turbot Inn, Mr. Kellow came to the door and said, "What's all this then?"

Someone in the crowd yelled out, "It's William! He survived the storm and he's come home!"

Mr. Kellow's eyes flew open, "William?" He asked, in disbelief, craning his neck to look at William more closely. "Can it truly be you?"

"In the flesh, sir!" William said, proudly.

"Well, do come in one and all," Mr. Kellow said, waving in the crowd with his entire arm. "Please, find seats. It is about damn time we had something to celebrate in this woe-begotten town! Melly!" He barked. "Tankards for ale and cider! Ale for everyone!" Melly, dressed in her blue frock with large sleeves and white pinny, waved to me and blew me a kiss and then rushed off behind the bar and quickly began to set tankards on the counter. As we entered the darkened, low-ceilinged room, our sanctuary against the rugged landscape and desolate moors, its familiar scents of crispy fried fish and pungent ale, all made by Melly and Mr. Kellow, welcomed everyone.

William looked over each shoulder for his companions

from the boat. "Everyone, please quieten down," he said, waving his palms towards the ground to silence the crowd. "First, this is surely the happiest day of my life." The crowd sighed and clapped. "I want you all to meet the people who rescued me, Captain Philipps and Dr. Tabb, from the *Charles Tucker*," he said with much esteem. The crowd hushed and turned to examine these new heroes.

"William, what happened?" Anne asked, pointing to his bandaged head. "How did you survive and what took you so long to return?"

"Well Mother, I owe a great deal to your floating coat that you made me wear that day," he said, kissing her cheek. We all waited in silence for William to continue. He drew a breath. But at that moment, a terrible *screech* from a chair that backed up on the floor causing all heads to look in the direction of the back of the room. Cade was getting up from the table where he had apparently been eating his midday meal with Jack Rowe, who had also returned from the storm. I froze at the sight of them.

"Yes, William, dear friend. Welcome back. Do tell us. What happened and where have you been while we have been here struggling to feed the town?" Cade said in a slight sneer as he slowly strode over to us. The gay atmosphere of the homecoming was shattered.

"You would know what happened, wouldn't you, Cade? Why don't you tell everyone here what you did?" William shot back, standing to his full height. He placed his hands on his hips. Captain Philipps, a muscular man in his mid-thirties, came around from behind William to face Cade alongside him. The air had become thick with tension as if everyone held his breath in dread and anticipation. The crowd's eyes darted between William and Cade in a mix of curiosity and unease. Knowing Cade's history, some eyed the door.

Cade's conflict-stained face stirred emotions buried deep in the minds of those present. Long held suspicions and ancient resentments that had long simmered beneath the surface, turned hushed mouths into whispers. The specters of past wrongs and perceived unfairness of the wealthy versus the poor seemed to hang in the air, woven with the scent of damp wood and stale ale. Cade's gaze, that of lowly local seamen with no prospects, met William's, that of a more wealthy, more intelligent outsider who could make his own options, directly in an unspoken battle of wills unfolding before the onlookers. Their rivalry, born of an ancient history of the class system, twisted like roots deep underground, and then crackled like lightning in the surface of the room. Each man dared and willed the other to break the silence with words that held the power to damn and fracture the other.

Knowing that I was a major part of the source of this crucible of emotion, brimming with unspoken conflict and unrequited desires, I thought I should intervene somehow. I felt we were all standing on breaking branches, slowly hearing the splintering before our weight would send us helplessly falling to irrevocable harm to futures that were fragile enough to begin with. I slowly stepped forward, my hand raised to suggest a calm, peaceful way forward.

"Effy," William said in a low, quiet warning without looking at me. "Stay where you are and don't come closer." I backed slowly away.

Every heartbeat seemed to beat as one, hoping that more

scars would not be made today as in so many of Port Quin's days past. But in that moment, as in the storm before it, a battle for supremacy was raging.

"I don't know what you mean, of course, William. Seems to me you have a bad head wound that gives you a poor memory," Cade scoffed.

William's response was quick and devastating. "You would know. You put it there. The day of the storm. You remember. You hit me repeatedly with a board, here on the forehead and here on the top of my head after I asked you to hand me the board to help me stay afloat." William's eyes flashed with anger. "What kind of friend are you who tried to kill me when men all around were dying? You sick bastard!"

"Not likely. How could I strike you when I was floating as well? I would have nothing to stand on to raise up and strike you. You were struck, no doubt, but not by me," Cade said, incredulously, pointing to his own chest. "Hallucinations, no doubt, from whatever did strike you. But I thank you not to blame me." He turned to chuckle with Jack, who was standing by his side, arms folded across his chest.

My mind immediately went to what I had heard on the wind during the storm. *I had heard exactly this.* How could I offer this as testimony? I heard this account on the wind during the gale. I would be locked up as a fool, a hysterical woman. And my father's ghostly account of the murderous one as I walked to the Carlyon house! How I wish I could scream that out at Cade now!

Anne, normally calm and collected, lashed out at Cade. "How could you do such a horrible, wicked thing, Cade? Trying to kill William? You will be punished!" She spat out, full of rage, shaking her fist at him. Others in the crowd were shocked by what they had heard, not knowing who to believe. Some muttered, "Outrage!" and "Trying to kill William!" in disbelief over what they had just heard. Tensions began to boil.

"As to the legal proceedings of this matter," interjected Captain Phillipps, "I suggest a full inquiry. We have taken down Mr. Carlyon's full testimony and I have it documented by our ship's purser on the *Charles Tucker.*"

"Yes, and his injuries are consistent with his testimony." Dr. Tabb stepped forward to say his piece. "I am a surgeon in Falmouth and came upon this young man as a passenger on the *Charles Tucker.* I was shocked to see this man almost die from the blows to the head and the subsequent bleeding. Had it not been for the lifesaving coat stuffed with cork that he wore; he would have sunk to the bottom or floated face down. I am willing to testify to that personally." He nodded with confidence; others in the crowd seemed to agree with the doctor. They turned back to William in what had turned into a court of public opinion there in the Turbot Inn.

"You heard him. Injuries that are like being struck in the head by another man. You, Cade. Not some other thing. You." William took several steps toward Cade. Other passengers from the *Charles Tucker* had wandered into the inn at this point and from their confused expressions, they obviously wondered what was going on. The local crowd visibly shrank back in fear of what would happen next.

A sickly, sinister smile spread across Cade's lips. "That proves nothing," he laughed. "Why would I want to kill you, William? You have nothing I want."

"Don't I?" William replied, eyeing me smugly. With that, Cade sprung through the distance of four steps between them and reached for William's throat with a fierceness born of generations of men of the moors. William blocked Cade's grasp with his forearm and a sharp jab in the gut. Chairs tumbled over. Women shrieked, and tankards went flying to the floor. Men were knocked to the ground in the fray.

The fight happened so quickly and furiously it was as if two male animals were doing battle over a mate in the wild. I had seen men brawl but nothing with hatred like this. Their faces were contorted in ugly grimaces, their teeth clenched. Cade struck at William, landing pummeling blows. William wrenched Cade's arm behind his back and shoved him up against the front door with a *crash.* Items on shelves along the wall burst to the floor, splintering to pieces. Anne and I clutched each other, paralyzed with fear. Cade reached into his belt with his free hand and produced a knife which he whipped into William's right hip. William let out a low yelp and thrust Cade up against the door with a final push.

"Let that be a lesson to you, Willie. No more false accusations." Cade threatened, out of breath and straightening his shirt. Jack tossed him his hat. Cade left the inn, laughing hideously. Jack followed with a sneer. William's eyes followed them to the door. Then he turned to look at his hip, pulling his trousers around to see the damage more clearly.

I ran to William's side in a panic, placing my hands on his back and hip, frantically trying to examine the cut. Panting from the exertion of the fight, he said, disgustedly, "Only a nick." A small red circle bloomed on his trousers. I pulled his shirt out of his trousers and bent back the waistband to look at the cut, which was only a small slice.

I pressed it with a wad of his shirttail to stop the bleeding. "Right. Just a small cut. No stitching required," I said to William as he stood panting from exertion. I glanced up from my kneeling position to Anne. We exchanged knowing glances. Cade's anger would likely not end here.

What had become clear to us all was that the night held more than just yet another rising wind and cloud cover—it held the promise of a reckoning that would shape our fates forever.

Chapter Eighteen

Cornish Magic

Port Quin, Cornwall, U.K.

August 17, 1841

I wondered when happier times would return, if ever. Mother and I sought refuge in the sanctuaries of our own bedrooms, retiring early that evening, seeking solace from the fight at the inn and trying to help the injured in the village still suffering from the storm that had long since passed. I wanted to forget the haunting whispers and specters that plagued my thoughts.

Every fiber of my being ached. I laid down on my bed in my white shift, craving the softness of my pillow and wondered if William was doing the same. I tried to think of happier events now that William was home. Home! He and Anne were entertaining Captain Phillipps and Dr. Tabb as house guests, and I imagined they both delighted in a welcome audience to discuss their ship building venture. I tried to calm myself by entering their ship building workshop in my mind. Such an intriguing, creative place! I imagined them sitting around and looking at the drawings and asking about experienced shipwrights. How William was born for this work! Now that he had returned, we could go over the contents of the paymasters' box. I wondered if Anne had told him she opened it. I saw the glittering, colourful stones in my mind…

But then I felt as if the atmosphere in my room had grown heavy and damp. A chilling, wet breeze blew a mist over me through the open window. I sat up in bed and squinted in the darkness. *Not again,* I thought. Suddenly I saw them through the mist that had entered my room. My father's ghostly face appeared and then his body in a gray vapor form and three of his crew stood at the far corner. Their hollow eyes were fixed on me. Terror coursed through my veins as I beheld their ghastly appearance and smelled their rotting stench. I tried to scream, but no sound came out of my constricted throat. I saw their cloudy forms as they stood tall and threatening, their hazy bony bodies wore tattered, wet sea garments strung with putrid smelling seaweed. They hovered in place, their mouths open and quivering.

My breath caught in my throat as the ghostly crew crept towards me. I backed up in my bed, cracking the back of my head on the stone wall. The pain revealed to me that this was no dream, and not another of my grim visions. Somehow, this was happening now, like the voice from the Bible I had heard during the funeral service. I opened my eyes wide in fear and desperation and said, "Come no further!"

I heard a cacophony of moaning, their words distorted. My father spoke on their behalf, "Surrender to my bidding. Avenge us! Kill the murderous one, the traitor seaman Caden

Bolitho!" As he hissed, his bony hand thrust out towards me, and I pushed my hands out in defense. I backed into the corner of my bed, hands remaining out.

I had never been more frightened, but in the depths of this fear, a spark of resilience ignited, and the words of Parson Hockings gave me strength. My voice quivered, "I have no fear of you! I walk with the Lord!" I mustered the strength to find my voice and hoped my mother would stay safe in her own room. My entire body was shaking with fear. "I will not succumb to your darkness. Not in life and not now!"

"We come to seek revenge and you will do our bidding!" Father screeched.

"I am not your instrument of revenge," I spat out through clenched teeth, shivering and clutching my arms about me.

The crew shuttered and cried out, shaking their bony jaws in anger at my words. My father jerked his head about in a tirade "The traitorous one Caden seeks to kill one of us. You must kill him first to avenge this disloyalty,"

I decided to use his past against him with the crew. "You were once my father's loyal crew, but did you know that in life he was unjust to his own family? Did you?" I shouted to them. "I seek justice, same as you. But I seek the light not through more death and vengeance."

Two of the crew howled in a terrifying chorus. My father's ghoulish voice turned darker, his hollow eyes narrowing to slits, with an unsettling and evil intensity. My attempts to defy him, as in life, only served to increase his chilling strength.

"Defy me, Effy," Jago my father hissed, his voice dripping with a haunting malevolence, "and your grandmother's life shall be forfeited. We have power you cannot begin to understand. I can drown her in the depths of my wrath. Drown her as she stands." He waved his arm in a violent motion, sending a water mist across my body.

My heart sank and a surge of terror coursed through my veins. In trying to protect myself, I had left him an opening to go after those I cared about most—my mother and grandmother, complete innocents, open for torture that I had sought to defy. I was paralyzed with fear. The weight of what I had just done pressed down on me, and I was left with no choice but to consider his bidding. My own defiance meant nothing to me compared to my love of my mother and grandmother. Or William for that matter.

Father's crew loomed behind him, glowering at me with their ghostly eyes filled with an unholy hunger. They silently affirmed their captain's threat; their menacing presence left no question in my mind of the power they wielded. They waited for my answer.

"If you are so powerful and could drown my grandmother where she stands, why don't you kill Caden yourself?" I asked.

"Silence! We don't kill our own, irreverent child," he moaned.

"I see. I can't allow you to harm my grandmother." I declared. My voice was shaking. "I will find some way to satisfy you if it means protecting her."

Jago nodded in agreement. His voice was filled with danger and delivered a clear threat. "You make a good choice. Remember, defy me and you will pay dearly."

As suddenly as they had arrived, the ship's crew dissipated. Their forms faded into an ethereal mist, until only the echoes of their presence lingered in the room. The air in my room was suddenly clean once more. I had tried to stand my ground against the onslaught of ghosts and defy them with my determination to forge my own path. But I failed. And I bargained with them. Was I insane? I was no match for this evil.

I ran to my mother's room. She was sound asleep in her bed as if she had heard nothing. I went back to my bedroom and pulled my day frock back over my shift. I coiled up the long braid that swung down my back and pinned it to my head. I quickly laced up my boots, grabbed my gloves, and strode over to the front door, and wrapped a shawl around my shoulders that had hung from a hook on the wall. "I don't care what time of night it is; I am going to Gran's to ask her why I have been hearing and now seeing ghosts."

My heart raced as I sought safety and guidance from my grandmother, longing for an explanation to unravel the knot in my stomach and the mystery of my father's haunting presence. With a mix of trepidation and anxiety, I ran down the street and knocked on her door, my eyes filled with questions that demanded to be answered.

She listened with her eyes closed as I poured out my gruesome experience, my voice trembling with fear and dread. Grandmother's face reflected a deep understanding of and compassion for the story and the wreckage inside me. She took my hands in hers, a gesture that spoke volumes about her belief in me and our bond.

"Effy, my dear," she began, her voice gentle and full of wisdom. "Yer faddur's ghost can only be seed by dem who be aware enough to hear and seed him. Most don't 'ave de ability. Yer muddur once had this ability but turned away from it. She closed her mind to it and turned to de Lord. The two ain't separated. I pushed her too hard on this and frightened her, I fear. I didn't want to do this to ye as well, which be why I haven't s'plained more of ye abilities to ye afore this. Can ye understand this, my child?" She asked, wiping stay strands of hair out of my face.

"Yes, but now I must know. I can't go on like this. Please, help me." I pleaded.

She nodded, completely understanding my urgency. "Your faddur's soul be tarnished wi' unfinished evil that lingers in the wake o' his passing. His spirit were strong in life and now be trapped between realms and can't find release. He wants to use ye to git the release his spirit needs. He needs ye earthly body to git he to the next realm."

"But I don't want to kill Cade and do his evil bidding!" I cried out to her, frightened. "And I am afraid. He said he would kill you by drowning if I didn't do as he bid."

Grandmother continued, her voice steady and reassuring. "Your faddur's ghost appears to ye because ye share the same strength and the same faults, somewha'. He seeks resolution via ye 'cause of this. But I fear he be clouded by pain and anger his early death left behind."

We sat on her thinly cushioned sofa and my mind was spinning with the implications of what she had just said. I yearned for clarity, and answers amidst all the tumult I was facing.

She continued, her wrinkled face still holding creases from the blankets as I had woken her up from a sound sleep moments ago. "Ye must remember that spirits, even those of ye parents, can be dark, very dark. The revenge will seduce even a spirit if t'is strong enough."

Just then a conclusion came to me. The missing girl Cornelia. Father had succumbed to destructive urges with Cornelia during his life. And it was likely that Cade had a run with her as well, later, probably based on Father's accounts of her delights. Cade was the one who dragged her off to Padstow and had his way with her under the threat of raping her mother. Cade was the culprit and Father was jealous of his forced conquest. Also, my father had never liked William, his fellow seaman, during his life, so what did he care if Cade had tried to kill William, other than a seaman's loyalty to one another? I had reached a kind of resolution that Father wanted me to avenge my poor William's attack, now struck me as mistaken.

A mixture of sadness for all of them, Cornelia, Father, and Cade—washed over me, along with the realization that I understood the gravity of the situation and the delicate balance between what must have been an attachment for Cornelia and his need to take revenge on Cade using William as an excuse. I also needed to protect my soul and future from the destructive path Father was oblivious and uncaring, was leading me down.

"Child, ye look as if ye know somethin'. Wha' t'is it?" Her voice softened, carrying with it the only form of reassurance I had.

"I am not sure, Gran. I don't understand it myself," I stammered.

"I offer this. Love comes in many forms. Trust love that lifts and brings the light rather than one that only binds. Seek to understand love that causes pain, for it cries out for calm. Hold onto the light within ye. Light be the true healing power."

"But Grandmother, aren't you afraid, like I am?" I asked her, reaching for her veined hand.

The look on her face told me that she clearly recognized that her safety was at stake, understanding that the lingering spirits and their twisted desires did pose a real danger if left unguarded. "We must remain vigilant and take the necessary precautions," she said, pointing at me. "We must create a shield, drawing on our ancient charms as a defense against evil. Together, we will prevail."

"But how? And what about Mother?" I asked, concerned and fearful that Father would come back at any moment.

"We need to remember our ancient practices. These be the things your mother pushed away long ago. But I can begin to teach them to ye now," she said, wringing her hands together, trying to remember the words and movements.

"I remember some chants you used to say when I was a little girl…" I drifted off. "I was often afraid, too, like Mother. But now I do want to learn. Teach me, Gran, so that I can learn to control my fears."

"Yes…yes…When in perilous waters, we draw from deep within, a sacred space, an inner voice that few possess. If we draw upon the power of our ancestral connections and the protective energies contained within us, we can safeguard our own interests and ward off the evil that the spirits hope to lure us with. The incantations be a combination of faith, grit, will, and conviction."

She stood in the candlelit room, waving her arms in fluid circles around her body and at times over her head. She wove words in and around these motions like a tapestry, creating a lattice of protection around us. "Our abilities be what we believe and what we make them," she offered in a hush tone. Her voice, imbued with a timeless authority despite her elderly body, began to resonate with ancient words, building the ancient shield against the vengeful spirits:

"By the power of blood and bone,
By the strength of spirits known and unknown,
I call upon the ancient line,
To safeguard our sacred shrine.

With words of wisdom I implore,
Open the gates and let light pour,
Banish darkness, let it flee,
Bound by love and unity.

From realms unseen, I beckon near,
Spirits lost come forth and hear.
With reverence I make my plea
Do no harm and set us free.

Ye spirits of hate and ye of dark,
I ward thee off, leave no mark.
By the light of love and truth,
Protect us now, our love and youth.

May my words be carried on the wind,
Peace and harmony descend within!
With this I call, and I stand,
Find only peace under my command!"

As she spoke these ancient verses, a sense of serenity filled the room, and a delicate peace scented the air. I felt the reverberations echo through the veils of time, reaching out to the supernatural realm that she and I could feel, see, and hear, establishing a protective barrier against spirits that sought to cause harm. With her incantation, she channeled the power of our pool of ancestral knowledge and connection that included Mother to harness unseen forces, directing them toward protection and harmony. I was thrilled to have a brief respite from the relentless specters that haunted me. In that moment, she and I stood together, united in purpose, ready to face the dark challenges ahead with strength and a touch of ancient, Cornish magic.

I kissed the top of Gran's head and bid her goodnight. I had to find a way to bring peace to my father's tormented soul before he destroyed the goodness left in mine.

Chapter Nineteen

NIGHT STALKERS

PORT ISAAC, CORNWALL, U.K.

AUGUST 17 & 18, 1841

The soapy scent of my grandmother's hair was still in my nostrils when we heard a sharp knock on the door. Gran and I looked at each other in confusion. I, for one, hoped that her incantation also applied to those who knocked rudely on doors too late at night.

As I opened it a tiny crack, Cade pushed in through the door, dressed in his Sunday best clothes. "Cade, what are you doing here so late at night? How did you know I would be here?" I asked, pushing him back through the doorway. "Grandmother is reading the Bible and doesn't want to be disturbed."

"Process of elimination," he said, speaking very quickly. "I brought some wine. I thought we could talk for a bit."

"Here, at my Gran's house?" I questioned.

"Well, no. I have a carriage. We could go for a lovely drive." He motioned in the darkness toward the street. I couldn't see anything in the blackness.

"A carriage. Late at night in total darkness? The only carriage in these parts belongs to the Castle. And I want no part of that, thank you." I said, shaking my head.

He insistently continued, pressing in against the door. "Come. Just a quick drink."

"Cade, no. I want no part of any drinking or any carriage ride. Now, good night." I pushed him out and began to close the door, but he grabbed me by the arm.

"I'll be quick and come out with it. I am dressed for our wedding. Please, will you marry me? I would like you to be my wife," he said, in a strange, strangled voice that sent shivers up my neck.

"What?" I shrieked. "No, Cade. I am sorry. I cannot marry you. I..."

"In that case, I shall see if you reconsider in the carriage." He pulled my arm roughly and clapped his other hand over my mouth, dragging me outside and down the street in the darkness. I kicked and fought with all my might, even though I was petrified. I bit down hard on his hand and ground my teeth together as the black form of the coach came into view.

"Damn you!" He screamed in pain, pulling his hand in to his body and shaking it.

"Help!" I screamed as loudly as I could muster, but it sounded weak and pathetic in the enormous darkness that enveloped me.

"I take it she didn't drink the wine with the morphine in it then." The voice was so familiar. A man's voice.

"No, and she bit me, the wench. Time for the chloroform," Cade said, his other hand now over my mouth and a new set of arms holding me from behind.

"I'll ask that you hand over the rest of the morphine I gave you then." Dr. Moyle said, out of breath as he struggled to hold me still.

"Not likely. Steady now." Cade took his hand down and I recognized the voice of the new man.

"Dr. Moyle! What are you doing?" A wet cloth covered my mouth and I suddenly felt extremely sleepy and limp. The cloth fell from my mouth but I dropped the man's arms, feeling so heavy that I could not lift my head or even a finger in my own defense.

"Get her into the carriage. I gave her a light dose. Only enough to get us to Port Isaac. She should just be coming out of it when we get to the Golden Lion. It will be crowded to-night. No one will notice a tipsy looking girl," I heard Dr. Moyle say. But it couldn't be Dr. Moyle trying to cause me harm. I was so confused, and my mind was so muddled.

"Yes, that is where the good Captain "Long," or whatever his true name is, agreed to meet us to perform our blissful wedding ceremony." Cade responded, sarcastically.

I could feel the carriage wheels start rolling as we got un-derway. I tried to protest but could not move my mouth. The two men were talking but I couldn't comprehend what they were saying except in bits and pieces. I understood "soddy cap-tain" and heard "take payment for the service." All I wanted to do was sleep but I knew I had to flee.

"She looks like a beautiful dream, just lying there, doesn't she?" I heard Cade wistfully say. "And I can tell you I have had a good many dreams about this one. I'd like to give her a good rodgering right here and now." I felt his strong hands creeping over my waist and up and over my bodice as he leaned across the seat opposite me.

"Good God, man. Have you no scruples at all? You are a sick bastard." Dr Moyle said, disgusted.

I felt my brain coming back in focus, but I struggled, still under the influence of the chloroform. I tried to move my feet so that I could stand and run at my first opportunity. I was truly afraid for my freedom.

"We should arrive in Port Isaac in a few minutes. Let's hope Captain Long is on time. Start shaking her to wake her up so that when we walk her to the Inn, she raises no eyebrows."

With that, Cade threw his body on top of mine and began to kiss me and fondle my breasts. "Oh, I know how to awaken her," he said breathlessly, laughing. I lay there frozen and could only clench my eyes shut.

"I want no more part of this, you hear. I am dropping you both off at the Inn and then I am leaving Port Isaac and Port Quin for good for parts unknown," Dr. Moyle said. "I won't have to worry about you trying to pin the grave robbing on me now."

Cade raised himself onto one elbow. "Thanks to you, I have the wedding bands that I need for tonight's festivities. That pearl pendant helped me make my case to Effy too, by the way." Cade remarked in a self-congratulatory tone.

"I never should have given you that pendant to shut you up about me selling Effy out to the party gents at the castle." Dr. Moyle sighed. "But she did bring me in a pretty penny."

Cade grunted. "Like you always say, 'Got to make a living somehow.' Your 'second incomes,' shall we say, were very handy for you until I found out about them."

"You and that snooping mother of hers. Mrs. Pengelly had to go tell Parson Hockings about the pearl pendant being from her mother's friend and now no more grave robbing. But there are many towns that are in need of a good surgeon and there are many more graves to rob, so I am not worried. Told my wife we have been called to a town that can actually pay for medical treatment, which is true enough."

"You didn't have to go and stab me in the leg when you were worrit I would tell our dirty secrets! We were able to come to an arrangement like gentlemen, now weren't we?" Cade remarked. His hand began to fumble at the bottom folds of my shift under my frock. I was able to move my feet and legs a bit more and I held them together as tightly as I could. I began to panic and my eyes filled with tears. *Oh Lord, please hurry horses and arrive at the Golden Lion.*

"How did I know you would keep your mouth shut? Thought you would need extra motivation. Thought for sure you would tell young Effy here about our adventures in the graves. Will you please stop pawing her?" Dr. Moyle pleaded.

"I think you like watching, old man," Cade sneered, pulling my skirts up and exposing my knees. I balled up my fist. "If you enjoy that kind of thing you would really enjoy the ladies up at the castle. They know their trade. I can tell you from first-hand experience."

"Certainly not," Dr. Moyle replied, adamantly rejecting the ideas. "We have arrived at Golden Lion. Straighten her up and make ready," he grumbled.

"Another time, soon, my love," Cade said, laughing in that strange, hideous laugh again.

"You, Cade, have got some form of brain sickness. Mark my word," Dr. Moyle admonished.

"I did use your words about brain injuries against William and that doctor of his at the Turbot Inn. Without your help I think they might have thought they had something of a case. But of course, they don't. So, I do thank you for that." Cade said as they pulled me out of the carriage.

"Another reason not to implicate me or I can turn right around and bury you, Caden, remember that." Dr. Moyle warned.

The two of them held me up by standing me up in between them. "Hold your head up, Effy, if you know what's good for you." Dr. Moyle hissed at me. We staggered into the doors of the Golden Lion looking like many typical patrons. They found a booth and slid me into it.

"I take my leave of you now, Cade. Good luck to you, lad." Dr. Moyle said, shaking his head, uncertainly.

I was so confused at hearing about Dr. Moyle's role in my capture tonight, my previous capture at the castle, and the grave robbing all at once. But as I thought back, despite my muddled state, to the surgery when he gave me that one long and knowing glare, I saw him clearly for the first time. What I had thought was a long look of admiration for my assistance was apparently an appraisal of my worth-what money he could get for me and whether I was naïve enough to not see him for who he really was. Which I did not. I did not see him for the conniving filth that he was. My faith in him and my dreams in the upper class and their cleanliness and forth righteousness were demolished.

"You were supposed to be a gentleman," I stammered at him with all the effort I could muster. Dr. Moyle looked down at me guiltily. "A man of the upper class. A man of honour."

"Upper class and privilege do have their advantages," he said, as he shrugged his shoulders, "and I simply made you part of my advantages." He tipped his hat to me.

"That's all I meant to you?" I slurred in disbelief.

"I saw a ripe flower there for picking. You can hardly hold it against me for plucking it." He strode off.

He had used me, him, from the upper class I had so admired, and badly. All the effort I had put into becoming more educated, to bettering myself so that I could crawl out of the mud pit that was Port Quin seemed ruined in that instant as I stared dumbly after Dr. Moyle. He cared so little for me that he traded me for money. Did the upper class really have no better morals or honour than a starving, desperate labourer, or fishmonger? I began to see how despicable the upper class could be, and it sickened me.

Cade was preoccupied. "And God speed to you, Dr. Moyle. I am off to find Captain Long." Cade took a few steps away from the booth toward the fireplace and looked to his right and left in search for the Captain.

As I sat in the booth, my head throbbed with the remnants of the chloroform, my vision blurred, and my senses dulled. A flitted-up woman passed too closely by me, looked down, laughing, and said, "My, we having fun, honey?"

Disoriented and overwhelmed, I slowly came to my senses, become aware of my situation in the back corner of the dimly lit pub, the pungent smell of stale ale and sweat permeating the dank air. As I sat leaning on the booth table, my heart raced with confusion and fear. How I had been duped! Cade with his "firsthand" experience! I could not be married off to Cade! I couldn't let Cade get away with this!

From where I sat, I saw the raucous fishermen at the end of the bar hoisting their drinks, their laughter echoing off the weathered wooden walls. The flickering candlelight gave their faces a warm glow. I could lurch forward to them and ask for help. But would they believe me? I rubbed my aching forehead with my fingers.

Through the smoky haze, I tried to focus my eyes, searching for my opportunity to break free from Cade. My mind raced to find some kind of plan while Cade was off trying to find the Captain. At the very least I could hide somewhere in the inn. I looked for a hallway or another door. I considered crawling on the floor under the table.

Suddenly, someone slid into the seat next to me. "Hallo, Miss. I see they be at it again. Trying to do 'e in, that is."

"What? Who are you? I slurred unintentionally.

"It's me, Tom, the carriage driver. I took 'e to the castle that time an' I just drove 'e 'ere. Never seen anyone run so fast that day in the rain. My mum be Mrs. Barrett. She seed them men pull 'e out o' the carriage and told me to fetch 'e out o' here. She be the one with the grocery store. The lady with no arms?"

"Oh, the shop keeper…how kind of her!" I tried to focus.

"Seems to me it ain't fair the way dem men are after 'e. I can help 'e escape. Follow me, quick like," he urged.

"Oh, Tom. Yes. Thank you. I have been drugged. I can't move quickly," I lamented.

"Take my arm. We must go quick." Tom urged, pulling me

by the arm out of the booth and towards the back door.

I reminded myself in that second of my love for William and our cherished dreams. In that tumultuous moment, my spirit burned with fierce determination, and I seized my chance to escape the clutches of Cade's sinister plan.

Our exit from the Golden Lion was a blur as Tom aided my escape. His calloused hand gripped mine tightly, pulling me through the back rooms. Our footsteps were muffled on the dirt floor of the kitchen, and no one seemed to care that we ran past. We darted through the kitchen doors and through washing tubs full of dishes, pots and pans hanging from the ceiling. Tom grabbed a knife off a chopping block as we ran by and hid it in his palm. We ran through a root cellar until we made it through to fresh air.

"Take it!" Tom said, thrusting the knife in my hand. "Know how to use it?"

"Not exactly," I answered.

"Best way is to thrust it in the kidney if 'e can git 'e arm round the man's waist, like so," he said, demonstrating on me. "From the front, grip it like so," he said, grasping the knife in his fist and forcing it in a downward thrust. He pushed me towards the street and said, "Run. Run as fast as 'e did that time in the rain. Go!"

"Thank your mum for me!" I whispered, turning to go.

"Run!" He hissed, pushing me on the back.

Port Isaac was a maze of tiny alleys with few lights as the port slept, casting shadows down upon my desperate flight. My heart pounding in my chest. I could taste the salt air as I ran directly for the opening to the coastal path just above the quays and back to Port Quin just above the harbour and directly across from the inn. As I emerged onto the quay, lined by small cob cottages where flickering candlelight danced in the windows, my determination grew with every footfall as I raced past these humble homes. In hindsight, I should have knocked on the first door I came to and asked for shelter for the night. I should have asked for help. But instead, all I could think about was escaping, putting distance between me and the inn and Cade and whatever captain would be heinous enough to perform a marriage for money. *Should I take the path back over the hills or the coastal path?* The hill path was quicker, but I would be less likely to run into anyone on the coastal path. My decision would cost me dearly.

Chapter Twenty

THE DANGEROUS GAMES WE PLAY

AUGUST 17 & 18, 1841

My instinct told me to race to the clifftops, the rugged coastline that veered upwards, away from the calming embrace of Port Isaac. I had ignored my instincts and my visions recently, so I felt that the coastal path was the right choice for my escape. I trudged up the beginning of the path, up the rocky steps and past the gorse bushes, up and up the cliffside, becoming quickly out of breath at the strenuous climb. The huge mass of the cliffs that lined Port Isaac Bay to my right reminded me of the strength I needed to make it back to safety.

As I reached the top of the cliff, the coastal path stretched out before me in the dark. I knew it was there even though I couldn't see it. I was breathing in ragged gasps, my throat burned, and my legs ached as I tried to put more and more distance between me and Cade. I could hear the surf below and to my right giving me a boundary in the darkness. The ground sloped down across the path towards the cliff edge and the surf, and I caught myself sliding and I had to grope along in the darkness for fear of stumbling over the edge and into the crashing surf.

How I despised Cade and Dr. Moyle. To think it was Dr. Moyle doing the grave robbing! Selling me out to the fishing party at the Castle like some common whore? Did he have no more regard for me than that? After all the hours of work I had done for him? I thought he admired me and my ambitions to learn healing. And Cade! Taking stolen goods from the graves! How lowly and despicable was he? To think he thought I would marry him because I was too dense to see through his lies. Was I that blind and naïve? My father and now these two men. How I loathed them. I trudged along in the dark, seething.

I couldn't tell how far I had gone, or how long it had taken me. I was creeping along more slowly in the dark than I would have done during the daytime. I tried to keep up my pace but was too tired, afraid, and exhausted. I sat down on a stone fence that I had sat on many times before, thinking about those that had sailed to the New World years before, like me, dreaming like me of a better life. I found a favorite large Gorse bush along the stone fence and got my bearings, feeling better about my surroundings even though all I could see were the white caps in the waves below and the outline of the stone fence along the path.

Then I began to feel the troubling feeling coming over me once more. All around, I could feel a cold mist, and tiny droplets stung my face and body. I shrank down on the grass, using the stone fence for shelter and instinctively grabbed some stones that lay on the ground for protection. The air smelled again of fetid seaweed and rotten, dead flesh. Through the darkness and haze I saw my father's ghost come into view from over the sea. His voice, tinged with sorrow and hatred, pierced the stillness. He was alone this time.

"Effy…" he urged. "The murderous one is coming. You must stop him." His words came across the wind. His hollow eyes and gaunt greenish gray face repulsed me and I looked away. As much as I loathed Cade, I was not going to rid the world of his influence by killing him. I dropped the stones and grabbed my knees to my chest. I was cold, thirsty, and tired.

"Effy, this is your calling," he said, his voice resonating with the echoes of the past. "Do not let him escape justice. He poses a great threat to your legacy…" I thought for a moment about that statement. If Cade came back for William again, my father could have a point. My voice caught in my throat as conflicting emotions surged within me. I longed for my grandmother's guidance.

The mist swirled around Jago, emphasizing his plea. His ghostly appearance with his seaman's clothes turned grey with rot and seaweed draped over one shoulder exuded a sorrowful determination. I knew this to be his unfinished business as described by my grandmother that would haunt us both. He grew angrier at my lack of response. "Remember your promise and mine," he howled, causing me to jump with alarm. I felt the anger he felt rising in me, and my heart ached with my choices, knowing that I stood at a dark crossroads.

"Your hatred comes from jealousy of Cade being with your Cornelia," I lashed out, feeling the anger surge within me.

"He comes to kill! He kills! Beware!" Father moaned and wailed loudly and then his mist evaporated over the sea like a cloud that simply blew away.

Shaken, I got up and decided I must get home as quickly as possible to alert William and the other men of Port Quin to the danger Cade posed. To my relief, the moon now shone brightly and I could see more clearly. I decided to heed my father's warning and took the knife firmly in my hand. I found the path again and began to turn on the bend towards Port Quin, more determined than ever to bring Cade to justice.

"Where you are going, Effy?" I turned and screamed, unaware that someone else was on the path. In an instant, Cade had put a rope nose around my neck and pulled it tightly. Knife in hand, I lashed at him with it, trying to stab his back and kidneys as Tom had shown me.

"Wicked bitch!" Cade yelped, wrenching the noose tighter, causing me to grab at the noose and drop the knife. "What have you got there? You nicked me!" He saw the flash of the knife on the ground and kicked it away, laughing. "Thought you would get the better of me, did you?"

I clawed at his face with my fingernails but he only pulled the noose tighter. I gasped for air as the rough rope scratched and burned the skin on my neck. He pulled upward on the rope and my feet lifted off the ground, kicking. My eyes were blinded with sparks of light. My jaw cracked and my spine popped. He dropped the rope and I fell to the ground, gasping for air and pulling the rope from my neck, even if only a little.

I was horrified and disoriented. "Cade, you lunatic! You're choking me! I can't breathe! Let me go!" I gasped, laying on my side as I fell. His sudden appearance out of nowhere shocked me, but his sheer strength and power left me terror stricken. I was no match for him physically; I was shaking from the pain he had caused me.

"Now, look what you made me do. You ran from the Golden Lion, and I couldn't find you. So, I had to think like you do. Run! Run home to William!" He said in a high voice, mocking me. "But now I have found you, haven't I? You are mine once again. You belong with me. And this time, I came with a rope, so you can't get away," he said with a sickly charming voice. "Don't worry, your little knife trick only gave me a bit of a scratch."

"Cade, why? Why would you want to hurt me?" I asked in a pathetic whimper.

"Oh, I don't. I don't want to hurt you. You will be my wife, don't worry. Once we find the treasure," he laughed shrilly. "Come along now, Effy. You are going to lead us to the treasure."

"What treasure?" I looked at him in disbelief and I croaked, my voice struggling from my constricted throat, shaking my head, and rubbing my raw neck.

"The one you are going to take me to. Now get up!" He pulled the rope with a strong yank, jerking my head and tightening the noose simultaneously.

I let out an involuntary yelp. "You're hurting me, Cade!" I cried, tears streaming down my face. I stood up as quickly as I could to avoid any further tension from the rope as he pulled me along, stumbling down the path.

Cade's demeanor had steadily changed over the course of the day and into the evening, I began to realize. He had become more and more demonic and out of his mind with loathing for

William and lust for money. He began discussing the Carlyons as a family of pirates hoarding treasure for years who killed anyone who became aware of it. I could see his eyes in the moonlight darting in all directions as he spoke. I was very unnerved by his irrational talk and knew that my father's ghostly warning was frighteningly real.

As Cade rambled on about how wicked William was, stealing treasure and killing people like his pirate father, I began to have another premonition. I could see the massive hole in the ground, the gug, that we referred to as children as "the giant's privy." In my mind, I could see the enormous black pit, almost like a cave but going down deep in the ground. We called it that because of all the giants in story telling in Cornwall, and played games around it, suggesting that anyone that lost the game would have to take a turn in the privy, a very undesirable place to be. The privy, in fact, was some distance but directly in front of Cade and I as he dragged me on towards Port Quin. I knew it was off the path ahead to the right.

Something dire was going to happen at the privy. I tried to let the premonition come to me, but I was distracted by the rope burning and digging into the skin around my neck, especially on the back of my neck. The pain was terrible, like wearing a necklace of fire or burning coals.

"I went to the Carlyon house to find you, you know. Took the carriage back there. No one was there but Mrs. Carlyon. She refused to tell me where that rotten pirate son of hers was. I asked her where the treasure was then. She wouldn't tell me that either," Cade rattled on, boastfully.

At this, my mind shifted to thoughts of poor Anne being subjected to Cade in his current state of mind. "So, you left and came to find me here," I said, hoping to keep him talking while I devised a plan to get the rope off my neck.

"No, I grabbed her by the hair and told her if she didn't tell me where the treasure was, I would slit her throat," he casually replied.

I was stunned. I paused my steps, only to be yanked forward by the rope. I wanted to scream out and wrestle away from him, but I had to remain calm. My throat tensed into a lump, and I was afraid to ask what happened next. "Cade, what did you do?"

"I dragged her around the house for a while, but I didn't find any treasure there. Then it hit me. The shed out back with the lock on it. She wouldn't open it but as luck would have it, she wore the key on her belt. So, I opened the door, and we went in. Remarkable drawings, I must say. Very talented for a group of dirty pirates." He laughed the same shrill laugh at his own sad joke.

"And Anne?" I asked. I couldn't image the torment she must have gone through. The pain and agony of being pulled around by the scalp. No treasure is worth that kind of torture, but I knew in my heart that Anne was ferocious in her loyalty to William and now to me. I knew without the need for any premonition that Anne would never give up any amount of treasure to appease Cade or give in to him in any way. I was trembling in a new way at the thought of my beloved, brilliant Anne suffering in any way at the hands of Cade, my once childhood friend now turned madman.

Cade turned to me and said, seriously, "I began to get tired of waiting for her to tell me where the treasure was. So, I did slit her throat."

A strangled cry leapt from my throat in anguish and my heart skipped a beat. I dropped to the ground and a low wail came from my throat.

"Cade, no!" I cried out in shocked disbelief and anguish.

"It was easy. Just like that lamb of yours," he said as if he was reporting on some ordinary chore, like chopping wood.

"You killed Moses?" I echoed, hoarsely, looking up at him from the ground.

Cade tugged on the noose to urge me along. "It was my mate Jack who did the deed but it was my idea. He owed me a favor. You were paying entirely too much attention to that gift of William's." He carelessly replied.

I blamed Father and all along it was Jack Rowe and Cade! I could feel the hatred I felt before surging upward from my innards to my heart and up through my mind. I wanted to strike him then and there with all my fury. But my reason took over. If only I could get him some medical help somehow, some rest. He would recover and face the accusations.

"Cade, you are doing terrible things and you need help. You have been through a hideous, tragic event that has broken your mind. Don't do this. Take the noose off and we can get help." I pleaded, stopping again.

"I don't want *help.* I want the treasure so that I can get out of Cornwall and away where no one can send me to prison. Don't you *understand?*" Cade shook the noose angrily in his clenched fist. His eyes burned with hate and his nose was inches from mine. In the pale light I could see sweat rolling down his forehead. "Nothing is wrong with *me,* only *you.* You are the problem." He yanked the rope forward and I lunged helplessly onward down the path at his side.

I must play him at his own game. Clearly, he has many weaknesses that I can prey on. Think! I screamed at myself. *Think like you did inside the Castle. What can I do to beat him at his own game…capture him instead of being the captive?* That's it. Game! I would get into his mind through his heart to free myself from this monster he had become.

Chapter Twenty-One

The Wind Whispers Secrets

North of Kellan Head, Port Quin,
Cornwall, U.K.

August 17 & 18, 1841

The moon cast a luminous glow upon the coastal path, its silver light reflecting off the undulating waves that crashed against the rugged cliffs. Whispering secrets, the wind blew as if it knew of the deceitful and fateful encounter that was about to unfold.

The weight of the noose constricted my breathing and caused open blisters on my skin, but I felt a strange calmness come over me, as if the noose would be gone soon enough. I traced the path that wound perilously close to the massive pit off to the right, leading to the tiny, unused slit of a cove. The dark abyss of the pit, which we had called the giant's privy, seemed to beckon me, a somber reminder of the dangers that lurked beyond us in the moonlight.

My mind raced, trying to create ways to outmaneuver

Cade and secure my own freedom without causing him too much bodily harm. I didn't want to kill Cade—only to somehow trap him. I resisted an unexpected urge to summon my father's ghost to aid me in my devious work. I thought of his ghost and an image came to mind. A horrible but very clear image of my grandmother gagging and grasping her throat as if drowning without water, just as my father's ghost had threatened. Was this happening to her now? At this very moment? Was this Father's way of making good on his threat since I was being firm and had not killed Cade for Father's revenge?

I created a cunning plan in my head and a voice to go with it. I put a smile on my face and said, in feigned childlike innocence, "Cade, remember how we loved to play games when we were little?" I jumped in front of him so he could see my face lit up.

"Umphf," he replied pushing me back.

"Let's play them again. Before we go to find the treasure in the cave off Port Quin." I dangled part of my plan in front of him.

"Cave? Which cave?" Fully alert now, he stopped and looked squarely at me.

"Play 'Over the cliff' with me and I will tell you which cave." I said, endearingly.

"No time for games, Effy," Cade grunted, pushing me back on the path.

"Too bad then. You will have to search all the caves around the Port then." I put my nose in the air. "Come on!" I urged. "I am taking off these silly gloves." I peeled them off as suggestively as I could and dropped them separately on the path. We walked farther. "And this shawl." I had his full attention now as I could see from the corner of my eye that his head was turned toward me. I pulled the shawl down lower on my shoulders and unclasped it and let it fall naturally to the ground.

"I want to run free like we did when we were children. I am taking my hair down too." Cade stood and watched me as unclasped my hair with difficulty due to the noose and then unbraided it. My auburn locks fell to my waist as I loosened my hair fully, combing my fingers through it. I could see his muscular body get weak with arousal at the sight of my luscious thick hair being pulled wantonly by the wind. "And you will have to take off the noose so I can run and hide," I said, flirtatiously, touching his chest with my fingertip. "Come on, Cade," I said in a sultry voice. "Don't you want to chase me?"

His eyes raked over my body as the wind flattened my frock tightly against me. Without the usual undergarments underneath, my frock pressed tightly against every curve, revealing all my womanly body parts. I opened my legs for effect. He came closer. I stood completely still tempting him with the bait.

Unable to resist, he took me in, hungrily. He came over to me and pulled me into his arms, saying, "You are all I have ever wanted." He engulfed me in a fervent passionate kiss, and I let him have his repellent way for several seconds until I broke free, panting. "The noose. Please take it off," I whispered, letting my face linger close to his.

Without thinking, he expanded the knot and pulled the noose over my head. He pushed his leg in between mine and I felt his manly response. Ecstatic, I said, "Let's play 'Over the

Cliff.'" My voice sounded suggestive and gave him my most flirtatious eyes as I skipped away towards the rocks at the cliffs' edge, my hips swaying. I looked backwards to see if he was following me. He was standing there, smiling, trotting slowly after me.

I began to chant the lines of the incantation my grandmother had taught me, if for nothing else to give me strength in a time of peril.

"With words of wisdom I implore,
Open the gates and let light pour,
Banish darkness, let it flee,
Bound by love and unity."

What would she do if she was in this situation? The only thing that mattered now is what I would do. Me. Effy. How would I use my own wit and bare hands to save myself and Cade without going into the darkness that I could feel my father drawing me into. *Stay in the light. Stay in the light.*

I found a boulder on the ledge and quickly ducked behind it, crouching down out of sight, giving the illusion to the untrained eye that I had jumped or fallen over the cliff. I could hear his heavy and eager steps behind me as he popped his head around the boulder and found me.

"Found you!" he exclaimed, bending down to put his hands around my waist and lift me up, my hair blowing all around us. He laughed at my playful spirit and bent down to kiss me hard on the lips again, which I permitted to ensnare him even more. His hands roamed my middle body as I made small encouraging sounds to blend the playfulness of the game with the thrill of our physical contact. He pulled at the strings of my bodice, trying to loosen them and he pushed into my breasts with both hands. My ample cleavage pleased his hungry gaze and I allowed him to bury his face there, but only for a second before I pulled away. The gravity of my hidden intentions was coming closer all the while. *Get him closer to the privy*, I thought, without him catching on. My heart pounded in my chest as I calculated my next move, my end game.

I pulled away once more and I started to run towards the privy with a dancing step. I ran faster and faster down the path towards the giant's hole. As I got closer, I could see that, waiting above the dark depths, surrounded by a deathly gray colour, not quite translucent but not opaque either, was my father's ghost and his crew. Their hollow eyes were hungry for revenge and their mouths hung open in the most sickeningly limp manner. I yelled out, "No Father, Cade is not to be killed, only captured." Father and his crew hovered over the hole, howling and moaning.

Father said, "I sent you the image of your grandmother. She did not survive. I warned you. You ignored my warning."

I stopped running yards from the pit to hear what he was saying. "You killed her? Gran is dead? Gran is dead?" I cried. I couldn't believe what I was hearing.

"I warned you. You will be next," he moaned, his bony finger pointing at me.

I was terrified and couldn't think straight. My poor Gran! My heart ached and I was out of breath. I wasn't sure if Cade would be able to see them in the mist or not. "Revenge us now or you die! Here in this pit of despair!"

"No Father. I won't kill anyone!" I began running again in

earnest.

"It is either you or your mother!" Father's ghost rasped angrily. To my horror, I began to have an image in my mind of Mother dropping a bowl and grabbing her throat in agony, bent at the waist, gasping for air, in the same manner as I had seen my Gran do previously. *No, not Mother!* My anger burned within me. *Didn't you cause her enough pain while you were alive?*

Glancing over my shoulder, I saw Cade catching up to me, so I enticed him with a weak and fragile smile. I turned and ran as fast towards the edge of the gaping hole looking for a safe ledge. At the last second, I turned back to see Cade again and caught a glimpse of his face contorted in a mixture of excitement and rage.

For in that fleeting moment, William appeared on the moor behind Cade, having deciphered the clues I left on the trail. His loud cries of my name pierced the night. Unaware that this was all part of my elaborate plan to have Cade fall into the privy, William ran towards us with galloping strides, desperation etched on his face.

Cade's eyes shifted from me to turn to William and then back to me with a terrible realization dawning upon him. He was following me too fast. I had veered away from the edge at the last minute. He looked down and saw his own foot over the edge of the giant's privy, too late to retract it. Eyes widened in horror, his legs wheeled around but with nothing under them and his footing faltered, the earth beneath him gone. With a gut-wrenching cry, he screamed, "Effy!" and he spun and fell over the edge, bouncing and tumbling head over heel over the inner ledges, disappearing into the unfathomable darkness of the gaping hole.

The ghostly crew hovered over the dark abyss, their ethereal forms illuminated by the moon's glow and the mist of the moor, turning them a foul green colour. Their hollow eyes had changed from vengeful to holding a grim satisfaction as they bore witness to Cade's demise.

Father slid forward in the mist; his voice uncaring of the life cut short. "The treacherous one has met his rightful end," he declared, his words dripping with ghoulish delight. "May his spirit find its own reckoning in the depths below." The ghostly crew swayed in an eerie unison; their eyes fixed on the dark void. Each one, their own lives also taken prematurely, exuded a sense of finality, and a release from unfinished business. In a collective motion, the ghosts formed a circle around the abyss. Father's ghost said, "Our effort is concluded. We will move to the beyond." With these words, the ghosts began to fade, dissipating into the night, as if they had never been there at all. Their murmurs of farewell filled the air in acknowledgement of the end of the tragic events and the final release from the earthly realm.

Silence fell upon the moor and the path, broken only by the echo of Cade's final plea. My heart pounded in my chest, a mix of relief and pain, for the game was supposed to end by Cade falling in deep enough to need a rescue, not by death. Sadness flooded my soul. The game had reached its ending, its consequences apparently irreversible.

The moon continued its solemn watch over the path, its soft light illuminating the aftermath of the fateful game. No sound emanated from the giant's privy. As William, filled with relief, stood at the edge of the hole, straining his eyes to detect any movement, his eyes met mine, and we both understood the gravity of what had transpired. In that shared gaze, we found solace, a glimmer of hope amidst the darkness.

I ran to William and he came to me. "William, it was an accident. He was supposed to drop onto an outer ring, not down to the bottom. Oh William, it is all so terrible!"

William looked into my eyes and saw the marks on my bloodied, raw neck. "Look what he has done to you! My God, Effy!"

My hands flew to my neck and gingerly felt my wounds. "Yes," I said hoarsely, "my entire neck is terribly painful. But your mother!" I cried, tears in my eyes.

"She lives, but only just. Thank heavens Dr. Tabb was here. He saved her life! We can't find Dr. Moyle anywhere and..."

"He's gone." I interrupted. "Dr. Moyle left town because he was the one coordinating the grave robbing. I heard it from his own mouth. Cade is dead," I declared with certainty. "My Gran too, my poor dear Gran." I sobbed.

"From the look of that fall, yes, he is dead. I can come back for Cade's body in the morning. I will bring men and ropes and retrieve him. But I am sure he is gone from us. And good riddance. Your grandmother? How do you know she is dead? What happened?"

"I will have to explain later," I sighed, wiping the tears from my wet face. "What of Cade's mother, his sisters? What will we tell them?" I asked.

"The truth," William said, without hesitation. "He lost his footing and fell. A grieving mother should know no more."

"How will they survive without Cade?" I wondered aloud, looking toward the giant's privy. "Give her the pearl necklace he gave me and explain to her how she can sell it."

"Perhaps you will want to give it to her yourself?" William asked, taking my hand.

"Yes, on second thoughts, that would be the thing to do. But oh, I dread it," I lamented.

"Yes, well, I would offer to help, but my being there would only aggravate the matter, I am sure. Oh, and my father has just returned during all this mayhem." William said softly, smiled and sighed heavily. "I am just so relieved I found you alive. You are my soul's calling. I love you, Effy. I want to tell you that again and again. I have that and more…so much to tell you."

"And I love you, William. With my whole heart." I wrapped my arms around his waist and laid my forehead on his chest.

The night whispered secrets, holding the echoes of my actions, what we had done and seen, our destinies forever intertwined by the moonlight scene forged on the that treacherous coastal path. With a heavy heart, I took one last look at the giant's privy, a childhood source of pretend hazard that had now become a source of real danger of the most final kind. A childhood friend whom I had hoped to save was beyond saving now and lay dead because of the games adults play. And who is to blame?

As I turned away, I carried with me the knowledge that I had been a part of something terrible but also extraordinary in its own way—a dance between the realms of the living and the dead, where vengeance found its resolution and souls found their peace. And I, what did I find? I had learned so much about so many, both brutal and beautiful, in such a short amount of time, not the least of which was about myself.

Chapter Twenty-Two

THE RECKONING

AUGUST 18, 1841

Charles Carlyon slowly entered the quiet of the Carlyons' sitting room and said under his breath, "I have just returned from the gug where the young man, Caden, fell. I offered the use of our wagon to take the body to the carpenter." He tossed his hat on a chair and looked at us, his eyes flashing. "Can anyone tell me what the bloody hell happened? Why this boy tried to kill my wife? With no warning?" His sharp words made me jump and I saw William flinch. "Well? Why was I not made aware of *any* of this until it was too late?"

William tried to begin to explain, "You see, Caden has been jealous of us for some time…"

I jumped in. "Caden has been suffering from a mind injury, a mind sickness if you will, since the storm and probably even before that," I explained. "Since you first arrived here he had it in his mind that you, because you are better off than some in town, are pirates with hidden treasure."

"Pirates?" Charles scoffed. He turned to look at Anne.

I pressed on. I didn't want William to bring up the contents of the paymaster's box here and I didn't yet know what Charles knew about the contents of the box. "Yes, and in his desperation, and with his affliction, he became violent." Luckily, Charles was more concerned for Anne than asking any more questions about the box, for the moment.

Charles walked over to Anne, knelt, and took her hand. "I guarantee you that he is gone. Dead and gone. He will never hurt you again. I blame myself for being absent too long." He looked broken, as if he would be lost without her, as he stroked her hand. They murmured to each other in mutually soothing tones.

Quiet returned to the sitting room and I resumed my examination with Dr. Tabb. "Any difficulties breathing, Effy?" Dr. Tabb asked gently, as I took deep breaths in and out. He had a bit of a limp and winced as he leaned over to examine my neck, I noticed.

"No, nothing like that," I explained. "Please, don't make a fuss over me. Mrs. Carlyon is in far more pain that I am." I smiled over at her, admiring her strength as she lay resting on a sofa by the large window in the sunlight, her devoted Charles by her side.

"Both of you need rest and plenty of it!" my mother exclaimed, bringing in some warm tea infused with willow bark for the pain. "Please drink this to lessen the pain," she said as she poured out the tea. I glanced at her wistfully, so thankful that she had survived my father's ghost's attempts to strangle her during the game with Cade at the giant's privy.

William had summoned Mother to his house upon our arrival, and while we rejoiced in our reunion, she and I cried together over the death of Gran. Mother had been living a nightmare during the time I was gone as Gran had immediately gone to her house after I had been so abruptly taken away in the carriage. The two of them had knocked on every door asking for help to search for me. Mother's eyes were red and swollen from lack of sleep and anguish, first over me and then Gran. She had been with Gran during Jago's ghost's rage and saw how he had drowned her as she stood, somehow with a ghostly force of water in her throat that could not be accounted for, which I had explained to her.

"I'm afraid your faddur's scars are etched deeply into our souls," she cried wrapped tightly in my arms as if she was afraid I would disappear again. And I clung to her, finding a semblance of safety in her embrace.

"I'm so sorry for Gran's death, Mum," I had whispered, full of sorrow and guilt. I tried to find a way using the Lord's light, but Jago was so strong.

"Ye did well, my brave girl. Ye're here, and dat's what matters now. We must go on, as strong as we can, mustn't we? And live our lives as happily as we can, as she would have wanted." She looked fondly down at me. Our grief for Gran was heavy to bear and unexplainable to anyone else. She had been a beacon of love and wisdom in our lives, and her absence was a painful void that Mother and I vowed to try to fill with love, rather than the hate of Jago.

"We will plan a righteous farewell for her with Parson Hockings, won't we?" she asked. I nodded; my head firmly nestled against her neck.

Dr. Tabb pulled me out of my grief and back to the evaluation of my neck injuries, which were extremely painful. "How about difficulty swallowing, Effy? Does your larynx cause you pain?" He touched the area gingerly.

"A little," I admitted. William had insisted that Dr. Tabb attend to my neck injuries immediately after we had found that Anne was getting some of her colour back. My mind wandered to Anne's horrible encounter with Cade. She confirmed Cade's heinous story about how he had tortured her over the treasure he assumed she had. When I asked her why she didn't just give Cade the treasure and have done with him, she responded, "I have lived my life. But you two have your whole lives ahead of you. Nothing and no one would cause me to spoil any opportunity for you." Spoken with true courage, I thought as Dr. Tabb continued to evaluate my throat. I wondered if I would have been that courageous.

"Effy, I have removed much of the blood and cleaned your open blisters. I have applied salve to reduce the pain, but you will want to reapply it four times a day. Keep the wrap around your neck for the time being and change it every day. Rest and allow the swelling to go down. You will continue to see significant bruising, of course." He nodded.

"Of course, I understand," I replied, looking into his eyes and noting something more that he wanted to say but was hesitating to do so. "There is something more, isn't there, Dr. Tabb?" I knew he would regret what he had to say next, especially to someone as young as myself.

"Yes, Effy. I have seen injuries such as this in other unfortunate victims...that is, what I mean to say is..." He fumbled to find the right words to deliver his message.

"What you mean to say is," I added in my most surgical tone, "is that some of the resulting red and purple spots or bruising in the skin will likely be permanent. And, I might even have no feeling in my skin in some areas. Is that it?" I asked, as stoically as I could. Mother gasped. Anne's eyes filled with sorrow.

"Yes, I am afraid so to both of those points. I am sorry to be the bearer of bad news. The good news is that your windpipe wasn't broken, and your voice will come back to normal." Dr. Tabb was a kind man and even though I had been taken in by his predecessor, I could not help but feel complete respect and admiration for him.

"I understand. No matter, Dr. Tabb." I replied.

"Dr. Tabb says I too will have a lasting scar." William pointed to the top of his forehead, still under white bandages. "We will all three of us have scars from the storm," William said, nodding to his mother.

"Your mother and I will wear collars and scarves and you, hats," I said with a croaking laugh from my recovering throat. "Mother, where are my knitting needles?" To that, Mother, Anne, and Dr. Tabb all laughed. I smiled. I didn't mind the scars of my trauma so much as long as the people here in this room were still alive.

"Dr. Tabb, you will recall me mentioning Effy's work in our local surgery. Perhaps you two would like to discuss your role aboard the *Charles Tucker?*" William suggested.

"Absolutely! I would be happy to discuss that," Dr. Tabb obliged, as he gingerly sat down next to me, holding out one leg. "Bad knees, you see," he said, grimacing.

I nodded sympathetically. "What I am most interested in at this very moment is how you sewed up Mrs. Carlyon's neck. What did you use and how did you manage it?" I asked, admiring her bandaging from my seat across the sitting room.

"Ah. Violin strings, my dear. An E string, to be exact! Much less prone to infection than silk!" Dr. Tabb relayed, excitedly, his hands in motion describing the process to my fascination.

"Now that your examination is over, Effy, perhaps we should depart for home and let Anne rest," Mother suggested, looking over at Anne, who was dosing off amongst her pillows.

"Yes, good idea, Mother." I agreed.

Mother and I stood and walked quietly over to the door and William shut it behind us. William gave a slight nod to Mother, and she drifted off toward the dining room. "Effy, before you go, I would like to reacquaint you with my father, who you haven't seen in quite some time. As I mentioned, he has returned from his trips to Bristol and most recently London. And, well, I have something to ah, well...explain to you. Something that my parents have already discussed with your mother."

"I see. It must be some matter of importance then. I would of course love to see your father," I said, eagerly. "I would like to express my admiration for his ship drawings and the workshop. Did your mother show you the paymaster's box?" I asked, excitedly, putting my hand on his arm.

"She told me she was able to open it but that she wanted you to show me what was inside," he said, hesitating.

"Yes, I can't wait to show you. You won't believe what..." William gently put a hand up to interrupt me.

"Yes, in due time. First, however, I need to explain

something to you, please. The box will have to wait," he said, firmly. "For now."

"Oh, I see," I looked into his blue eyes, which were a bit worried and downcast. "Something is wrong."

"Not wrong, exactly." He pulled me gently aside into the hall by the stairs. "Please, sit down while I explain something to you." We sat in two straight backed chairs with cream-coloured cushions near the stairs, while alarm bells went off in my head.

"I am going to tell you what I tried to tell you that evening when we were alone on Kellan Head. That was the night we found the box. I told you that I am not perfect by any means. I have made mistakes. Do you recall me telling you that?" He asked, looking down at me, with his handsome face and loving eyes connected to mine in a strong and solid expression.

"I do recall you telling me that, yes." I could tell he was about to tell me something unfathomable, but what, I couldn't imagine.

"Effy, I promise that I will tell you the truth, always. Because I love you with all my heart." He looked at me and nodded. My eyes searched his for clues as to what he was about to tell me. "A little over a year ago, when we lived in the north, I met an older woman who took a fancy to me. I was nineteen at the time and had never been with a woman before. I had never even walked out with a woman," he shrugged. "Please believe me when I say I did not love this woman, but she believed my family had means. I never drunk alcohol before—you know that abstaining is the Methodist way. Well, at least, I hadn't drunk in any *significant* way. But, one night, she plied me with drink. Hard liquor. One thing led to another, and we…we…" His voice cracked in shame. He looked down at the floor and he folded his hands together, gripping them tightly. "We lay together one time because I had stupidly had too much to drink." He said quickly, forcing out the words, swallowed hard and bit his lips together. He reached out and took my hand and I felt the anxiety he felt through his sweaty hands. I was shocked. I braced myself by clenching my stomach. My mouth was completely dry. I too looked at the floor. I prepared myself for what he was about to say. My heart felt like it was being cruelly crushed by a hammer.

"She has come for you with her child," I said, my bottom lip quivering.

"No. No. She died in childbirth," William said, with a giant exhale. "She's gone. But that one and only union did result in a child. And my father has found the child. Her family is all dead and gone as well. Cholera. My parents felt a Christian obligation to the child, despite his being a bastard and the disgrace of that and I do as well. He's a boy. A fine boy, Effy. He is upstairs and I want you to meet him."

"I see," I said, trying to take in the blow. I stared at my hands in my lap.

"I don't even remember the night it happened," William said, softly. "I am so sorry to tell you this now, after all that you have been through, and that I shock you."

"How can you be sure that it did happen and that you are the father?" I asked, logic taking over.

"All I can say, and I have been over and over this in my head, is that circumstantial evidence suggests that it was me and that I am the father. I take full responsibility." William said.

I sat for a moment, relieved that the mother was not a threat but also gripping the reality of a child. After a moment, tears in my eyes, and still somewhat in disbelief I said, "In that case, you have a son."

"Yes. Do you despise me? I understand if you do and you no longer…"

"No, I don't despise you, William, and never would. Can I see him?" I asked, recovering from my initial shock.

"Of course," he took my hands and pulled me to my feet. He held me in his arms so warmly and tenderly and then said, "Father is with him upstairs."

I nodded. He took my hand and we walked up the first few steps. I paused halfway up as I followed William. "What is his name?" I asked, some of the initial shock wearing away. "I'd like to know his name before I meet him."

William turned to look back at me from higher up on the staircase. "Mother, Father and I would like to name him William," he said. "Will for short."

"That sounds like a fine name," I smiled, looking up at him. "And what of his middle name? What will that be?" I asked.

"I have an idea for a middle name but would like to discuss that with you. That is, if you think it would be acceptable to you." He smiled and we walked the rest of the way to what had now become the nursery hand in hand.

Chapter Twenty-Three

THE SHADOW'S EMBRACE

PORT QUIN, CORNWALL, U.K.

AUGUST 20, 1841

"Though she's died, she isn't gone. I feel her all around me," I said to Mother as, dressed all in black, we prepared to begin the long march to Gran's funeral. I pulled at the lace collar on my dress, which irritated my bandaged neck even though I had left several of the top buttons undone but covered up by a cleverly coiffed hair style. Mother seemed preoccupied in the transactions of the event. Having paid the town carpenter, who was also the undertaker, thirty shillings, which she found hidden in my father's belongings, to make the pine coffin, she now examined it outside the window of our living room. The box was stained with a rich dark cherry with two heavy rope handles, one on each side and a large, enameled plate on top.

"I believe folks can smell the coffin varnish for miles around. Nothin' draws a crowd like a buryin'," Mother said, tired from a long evening of hosting "the watch" of Gran's body the night before which included saffron buns and ale that Mother and I had made, with the help of Melly and Mr. Kellow, and my aunts, who had stayed long into the night. All our friends and neighbors were there, including my brothers of course, who skulked about looking guilty for their lack of time spent with Gran.

My intention during the evening watch had been to give the pearl necklace to Cade's mother and sure enough, she was there. She looked worn and frail and Cade's three sisters roamed the house with empty eyes.

"Mrs. Bolitho, I want to give you this necklace, which Cade gave to me a few days ago. It could fetch a healthy sum...for future needs." I pressed it into her soft hand. She looked down on it but had asked no questions.

"He loved 'e in his way, that's sartin'," she had said, eyes watering and her hands shaking. "He done no wrong 'cept to love 'e."

"Yes, I know." I had closed her fingers around the pendant and chain and held them fast in my own.

Mother's shoulders were in a bit of a tired slump and she sighed as she looked out the window again at the carpenter's cronies who had agreed to carry the box. most likely for a shilling at the end of the journey or perhaps for a portion of liquor. The four bearers stood waiting outside to take their places around the coffin, one at each side with the carpenter at the head, as had been done, handed down through generations. No horse-drawn carts or carriages were ever seen at a funeral. The box was always addressed with deference by hand. They waited to lift it on to their shoulders and set out on their three-mile journey to St. Minver.

As was always the custom, the carpenter as undertaker came to the door and said, "Well Jinny, hast ye got any liquor? The chaps out there's a little afraid."

As the Cornish were universally afraid of the dead and dreaded anything to do with them, this exchange was expected and typical. "Yes, my son, plenty, plenty," came Mother's commonly given response. I suspected that since the coffin held no less than my Gran, a known user of the dark arts, their fear was somewhat heightened, and therefore a little more liquor than usual was required.

To my mother's response, the undertaker turned to the bearers in front of the house and said, "No fear boys long o' Jack. Jinny's got plenty o' liquor!"

The bearers then cheerily replied, "All right, Tommy, we can stand in now!" And with that, they began to sing our most cherished and mournful Wesleyan hymn.

"Where'er we go, where'er we be,
We're marching to the grave—"

The crowd came from every direction as no work would be done for miles around on a funeral day despite losing many after the storm. Nothing drew a crowd, not even a festival or a holiday, like a funeral of even the lowliest man or woman of Cornwall. The assembly never numbered less than many hundreds and was attended by many cousin Jacks and cousin Jinnies, as all the Cornish were called. Everyone came and chanted the hymn as they joined us in the march to St. Minver.

I could see the tall spire of St. Minver's as it came into view over the hill in the distance. As we trudged up the path, and came closer to the grey church, I saw Parson Hockings waiting for us at the head of the grave. Hordes of people, all dressed in black, and many of them women, were there to pay their respects to Gran.

The sun beat down on us as the mourners gathered around Gran's final resting place. The bearers sweated mightily after the long journey, and I imagined were only too thankful that Parson Hockings indicated with his hand that they could lay the coffin on the ground next to the grave. He began to say his final words and some of the carriers wiped sweat from their faces with their handkerchiefs. I too felt the heat of the day as a small stream of sweat dripped down my back through my shoulder blades.

The afternoon sun cast long, stretching shadows across the side of the church and the headstones before us. I noticed that the shadows of the nearby graves and trees seemed to elongate. The shadow of Gran's tombstone also elongated, taking on a formless, ethereal silhouette at first, but then began to bear a striking resemblance to Gran herself. I forgot all about the heat and became greatly afraid of the movement of the shadows.

The mourners, lost in their own grief, were oblivious to this supernatural occurrence, but I was entranced. I watched, my heart pounding as the shadowy figure drew closer and closer to me. I wondered if Mother to my right or William, standing directly behind me, could see any of this or noticed my agitation as the shadow drew closer to me. I began to shake with fear. Was this real or imagined?

Then a wind came up around me in a strange and unusual

form, like a swirling banner, and in it I saw the faces of the seafarers who had perished in the fateful storm. Where before I had seen their faces etched with pain, now I saw them one by one at peace, flowing around me, first low then higher up in the air, on the breeze, sifting through the crowded bodies of the mourners. I became calmer as their faces were as I had seen them in life. Each face showed clearly against the black mourning clothes as they slowly ebbed by in the puff of air. I marveled at this wonder and considered that it could only mean that my former friends and neighbors had found peace, which filled me with happiness.

The shadow seemed to murmur to the faces on the banner and they smiled and nodded at her in return. And then slowly, the shadow came through the banner towards me. All at once, it merged into my own body, sending a shiver down my spine. In that instance, I was overwhelmed. I experienced a flood of memories of Gran and I playing in the fields and at the beach when I was a child. Of baking bread and taking stew off the stove. I saw flashes of Gran's entire life played out before my eyes—her childhood, meeting my grandfather, her wedding, holding my mother as a baby, and her moments of confusion with what were her early experiences with her premonitions. Fleeting glances of secrets she held within her.

As I watched the carriers lower the box into the grave, I felt a warmth of confidence build within me that I had never felt before. A kind of understanding began to grow within me in terms of my Gran's mystical abilities. I could feel a power course through me like a dormant wellspring of magic awakening within my very soul. My grandmother's knowledge and talents in the dark arts were not dark after all but a kind of heightened awareness and another form of intelligence that I didn't know existed. And that intelligence was now part of my being and I felt I now had the ability to harness these powers. I couldn't control them but I was now aware that they were there.

Within moments, the shadowy figure completed its transfer and dissolved out of me entirely and formed its own shadow again. Then it drifted back towards the grave and sank into the box, leaving me with a profound sense of connection to my grandmother's legacy and newfound abilities and confidence to continue her work to promote goodness through our ancient knowledge of promoting faith and light. Unknown to the mourners, I had become the inheritor of Gran's superior abilities and my life would be forever entwined with the enigmatic world of magic and mysteries that was Cornwall.

I heard gasping and felt something hard beneath me. My left shoulder and side hurt painfully.

"Right strange," a woman muttered.

"Strange as her Gran," another whispered back.

"It's the dark arts! I seed her use it afore at the Castle!" I turned my head to see the girl with the curly hair from the Doyden Castle nightmare pointing her finger down at me. A man pulled her back into the crowd.

"She's only fainted. From the heat," I heard Dr. Tabb say in an annoyed tone.

"Effy, can you hear me?" William said, his strong arms propping up my back as I lay limply on the ground. I felt my head roll to one side. I attempted to lean forward a bit, bewildered, opening my eyes and lifting my hand to rub the pain in my shoulder.

"She's alright. Overwhelmed by her Gran's passing that's all," Mother said, on her knees with her hand on my cheek and looking up at the crowd, attempting to placate them. What seemed like thousands of dark eyes looked down on the three of us full of alarm, fright, and dread.

Chapter Twenty-Four

Don't Speak Ill of the Dead

August 21, 1841

The following day was Cade's funeral. I had decided to seek out Cornelia at St. Minver's but she was nowhere to be seen. I had made my mind up and was determined that she and I should not go on separately, alone in our knowledge of what he had done to us. That together, perhaps we could forge some type of solace that only she and I could fathom.

I went unannounced to the grain mill that she and her father operated, lest she refuse to see me. The timeworn greystone walls of the mill were covered in moss, just as they had been for a century. The slate roof had aged and weathered and bore the marks of countless repairs from scores of storms, a testament to the hardworking, enduring spirit of its residents. A few pigs greeted me in the yard. The mill straddled a lively stream and its large wooden waterwheel creaked and groaned with age, a marvel of engineering. The huge wheel turned with unwavering determination, capturing the power of the water and channeling it through its wooden maze of gears and shafts. I found her there, hard at work, under her father's watchful eye.

Cornelia, her father, and a few workers in rough-hewn clothing carried heavy sacks of grain to the massive grinding stones. Others loaded it into the hoppers, making sure each kernel of grain met its fate. Flour dust hung in the air, creating an atmosphere of cloudy mist. I watched in awe at the dedication of both mill and worker, transforming the harvest into much needed sustenance for the people of Port Quin. I thought the scene was much like the harvest at sea—dedication, skill, the right tools—and our reliance was equally on the sea and the land.

"Cornelia, a word please," I called out, motioning her over with my hand. She wiped her hands off on her apron and looked at me sideways and cautiously. "I didn't see you at Cade's funeral, so I thought..." I stammered.

"Folk gotta eat," she replied, as she swaggered over, placing her hands on her hips.

"I imagine you have hard feelings against Cade. Understandable," I said.

"Not right to speak ill of the dead," came her quick reply and she turned to walk back to her work.

"Wait, please. Cade told me what he did to you. I am here to tell you he also hurt me. Look here." She glanced back at me. I pulled down the collar of my frock to reveal the white bandage around my neck. Her eyes flew open when I revealed the remains of Cade's carnage underneath. She stared in silent horror. "He told me what he did to you as he did this to me. With a rope."

"Why? He told me you two was to be wed," she said, arms limp at her sides.

I shook my head. "No, that was never the case. I believe Cade was sick in the mind. And the storm made it worse. Much worse. That is why he hurt you the way that he did. And that is why I came here. So that you wouldn't feel alone—like you were his only victim or that him hurting you was your fault. Do you see? You did nothing wrong."

"He said I deserved it. He said he would do the same to my Mum!" She hissed under her breath so no one could hear, even though the din of the mill clearly covered up our conversation.

"You didn't deserve it, no matter what Cade said," I soothed. "You and I must be strong and carry on knowing that we did nothing wrong, do you understand? What happened to us was not our fault." I looked into her eyes to see if my point was reaching her, but clearly she was not hearing my deeper meaning.

"But what if..I am fearful that I am with his child." She looked at me full of shame and remorse, tears filling her eyes. "You know healing. Is there a tea I can drink or a tincture of something to get rid of it?

"I do know of some herbs that can be brewed in a tonic, but only a doctor is allowed to give them. You would have to get them at Port Issac now that Dr. Moyle is gone. How do you know it is Cade's?" I asked, dreading the answer but I had to ask it now or never.

"I beg yer pardon! What do you mean by saying such a..."

I raised one gloved hand. "I know you were with my

father," I said, my eyes cast downward.

"But, how could yeu know this? Cade?" she sputtered.

"Yes, and I saw you in the barn together. No use denying it any further and we will not speak of it again," I said.

Cornelia sat down on a nearby stone, suddenly very limp looking. "I loved him, ye know. He fancied me. Told me I were pretty."

I let her comment sink in before I responded. "My father, your father, Cade, Dr. Moyle," I slowly said. "They all got what they wanted when they wanted it from us women. And we as women must bear their behavior, whatever they choose it to be. Is that what love is? We must learn to stand up for ourselves and what we want, Cornelia, as part of this rugged life." With that, I warmly squeezed her shoulder. "Many are leaving Port Quin. What will you do?"

Cornelia looked weary, as if her father worked her to the bone. "Dunno. Not so easy to move a mill, your whole life," she said. "Ever wonder what upper class ladies do all day?" Cornelia sighed, as if in a far-off dream.

"I don't know, but I imagine them in a kind of delicious solitude. My guess is they don't make withy pots from saplings and nuttall branches, which is the work that now awaits me," I replied, looking down first at my red, chaffed hands and then at her hands which were red, rough, and cracked as well.

"No, they wouldn't want to foul their white gloves," she said, as if in a dream. I left her sitting there in the heart of the mill, with the sound of rushing water and whirring machinery like a soothing methodical beat resonating through the air. As I walked away, I left wondering what her life would look like in three months or a year. Life was hard for a woman. Harder still for an unwed mother. Many an unwed mother would kill themselves or be found buried at lonely crossroads. Would her father hide her away as was often done? I knew she had grit and was a survivor. I would see her again. What would any of our fates be, and how would the strength of our dreams be tested?

Chapter Twenty-Five

BOUND FOR RICHER WATERS

PORT QUIN, CORNWALL, U.K.

AUGUST 21 – 24, 1841

"Ye heard Dr. Tabb. Ye must rest, Effy." Back at home, Mother watched over me to make sure I recovered inside and out from my terrifying ordeal. But each day, more and more of the residents of Port Quin were packing and moving to nearby towns, which made Mother and I anxious and didn't help our recovery and mourning. We had many questions but few answers as to our own fate.

Melly and Mr. Kellow came by to drop off some of his saffron buns that I so enjoyed and to see how we were getting on. I hadn't had any of those buns since that day Melly and I went to set up our lobster pots together. That was only a few days ago but it felt like a lifetime, since so much had changed since the storm. Everything was different now.

Mr. Kellow was our window on Port Quin as he filled us in

on the latest news that he picked up from the inn. "Some folk be movin' to Padstow and then emigrating to Canada for work. I hear plenty of them saying that they be tired of chasing the pilchards and that there be fish a plenty in Canada, so they be bound for richer waters," Mr. Kellow relayed to us over supper at our house.

"Canada!" Mother replied. "So far."

"Yes, even the miners be tired of trying to find work, I be sartin. Business at the inn be declined sharply. Melly and I been thinking 'bout our place as well, ain't we, Melly?"

"Yes, Pa. More folks been goin' into Port Isaac, so we be thinkin' of startin' a place there. We be thinkin' ye might like to join us. Work together there to build a new Turbot Inn." Melwynn looked first at Mother and then at me, hopefully. "Maybe Willy and his family would like to move there too with their ship buildin'." Melwynn had clearly thought this out in her mind. "Port Isaac be a wider and deeper port, better for bigger boats."

"A wonderful idea, Melly, truly. Something to consider..." I replied, hesitantly. "I am not sure what William's plans are, for he and Will..." I trailed off. Mother and I had decided to talk about William's son Will with no fear of social disgrace about his origins.

I thought back to our conversation after I had met Will for the first time just days ago. Mother and I had walked back home from the Carlyon's slowly. "I see it on your face that you are in love with two now, Effy. First William and now baby Will," I recalled her saying.

"I don't deny it. Will is a divine angel," I replied, smiling at her.

"I daresay at your age, your mind and body are likely naturally yearning for a babe like him," she said, thoughtfully, as she held a basket of bandages for my injured neck and some food Anne provided. "Keep in mind, he is not a puppy."

I laughed. "No, but I think he will be well attended by all who know him like he is one." We giggled at the thought of Anne, Charles, William, me, herself, and others who had all argued over who could hold him next while we were at the Carlyon's.

"Effy, him bein' a bastard. It won't be easy." She said looking at me with all her good motherly intent.

I sighed. "There is much stain in this world that will be attached to him. But I will have none of it. We will manage it somehow. I plan to support all of them and love Will regardless. What say you?"

"Exactly, my darlin'. I say the same," came her reply.

We smiled at each other but our smiles quickly fell from our faces as we turned the corner past the Turbot Inn and saw Jack Rowe leaning against a tree. His dark eyes surveyed me up and down.

"You seed that bastard child, ain't ye? Yeah, I heard 'bout it." He stared at us in an ugly, threatening way. I paused and Mother pulled at my arm to continue walking. Instead, I put my basket down and walked directly up to him.

"You are grieving Cade's loss. We all are," I said, standing tall and spitting my words in his face, much to his surprise. His breath was sour from ale and his teeth were yellow and brown from lack of care. "But I will not have you marking an innocent babe with your hate. You who have no higher birth than him. Throw stones at him, will you? You will have me to answer to." I narrowed my eyes and thrust my chin out at him. His eyes never left mine. He cracked his knuckles in a menacing way. Livid, I spun around and strode back toward Mother and snatched up my basket, never looking back.

Lost in thought remembering this long-coming confrontation with Jack, I missed part of the conversation we were having at the table with Mr. Kellow. "We could use your wonderful rabbit stew on offer, Mary," he was saying. "You know how much my customers love it and your honey ale. I would value having ye to work with, you know that," he added. I could see a spark clearly lit in Mr. Kellow's heart for my mother. His face was glowing just looking at her. And why shouldn't it be? She was a wonder among women. Lovely and warm hearted, intelligent, and kind. None better.

"I must say I like the idea very much," Mother blushed at his compliments. "And I have always liked Port Isaac," she replied, looking at me. "Effy likely be pulled in a different direction, and she has her own life to lead, much as I would love to have her with me." She patted my hand. "But Mr. Kellow, how could ye find and afford such a place now to even consider such a thing?"

I was thrilled at the possibility for Mother. She would be able to put her skills to good use and with purpose. But more importantly, with John Kellow, a man who was forthright and kind, who had always seemed to value her as a woman for her talents and for herself was truly remarkable. I would not get in the way of this opportunity for her but I wasn't sure this was the path for me. But hadn't Mother and I said we would get through life together? And what about William and little Will? Where would they be? The course of events was all too overwhelming for me now.

"Leave that to me to investigate. I will see what be available and what we can make of it." Mr. Kellow nodded. "But let us not get our hopes up just yet. We must be savvy and shrewd in our business dealings. As in life."

"That is not to say that we Carlyons aspire to be the great family of shipbuilders like the Hilhouses who build for London owners; we don't. Our vision is to build for local buyers who want to trade with France and Ireland rather than Cyprus and Mauritius, Calcutta, and Sydney—that is, at least to start with." Charles Carlyon sat before the fire smoking his long-handled pipe after supper, discussing his most recent trips to London and Bristol, Bristol being one of the busiest ports in all of Britain, full of prospective customers and supporting a big ship-building trade.

I sat admiring him, while I was holding sleeping baby Will, in my arms. I was listening intently, along with William, who stood by the fireplace, his forearm resting on the mantlepiece. Anne was upstairs, still recovering from her injury. Dr. Tabb had insisted on staying an extra week or two to make sure the wound did not become inflamed and was teaching me how to continue to properly care for it. Some of his teachings I already knew and he was impressed with the care I was able to provide. We formed an immediate bond over sterilization, the use that had been made of violin strings, and signs of the wound becoming inflamed. He also taught me several new points about infant care, which of course Will needed. I relayed to him what Dr. Moyle had taught me and he agreed with it entirely; despite Dr. Moyle's lack of integrity, he had been a fine surgeon.

As we sat around the charming fireplace Charles Carlyon stood as a sterling example, I thought, of Cornish resilience. His sturdy physique was the frame of a gentleman but wore the garments of a more simple and humble man. The lines in his face were seasoned and gave the impression that no one should challenge him recklessly, as he bore the marks of time and toil, his skin weathered, telling the tales of countless days under the radiant Cornish sun and many nights huddled over his detailed drawings of ships. Only the sandy colouring of his hair, like his son's, made his appearance unusual for a Cornishman.

I studied his eyes as he continued to ask questions about how the use of steam engines had become popular in ship building in new ship design. They held such a spark of underlying curiosity. A testament to his intellectual prowess. They flickered with keen interest as he listened attentively to Captain Phillips' insights into the likelihood of steamships becoming universal.

"Captain Phillips, do you see steamships as the coming thing or will sailing ships still be wanted, do you think?" He asked the question but I could see in his eyes he already knew the answer. Captain Phillips needed no time to reply.

"Steam certainly but both will increase but with passengers in mind," he said, nonchalantly.

I was more interested in observing Mr. Carlyon than listening to Captain Phillips' response at this point. While I didn't know Mr. Carlyon well and this was my first real encounter with him, I felt as if his mind was like a sharpened blade, constantly dissecting and analyzing the opinions of his companions gathered around the fire. In truth, I realized that he may not have many such opportunities. Amidst the animated conversation, the occasional puff of their pipes, and the crackling of the fire reflected the inner passion he seemed to turn over and over in his mind what ship owners would desire in trading vessels as time went on and what implications that would have for his designs. *The humbleness of his demeanor belied the intensity of his thinking and spoke volumes about his wisdom and vision. Very much his son,* I thought.

Despite his keen intellect, the question at the core of the success or failure of the venture for me remained. How would he, with his lowly origins, convince prospective buyers that he was a dependable ship builder? I doubted whether he had had any significant education. What was Mr. Carlyon's intention: to be seen as an equal, a peer, of a buyer who would obviously be a gentleman or person of substance and influence while he was not? I was more than intrigued by this question as it went to the very core of my own ambitions. And while I certainly had no education at all, I tried to learn as much as I could about healing—its terms and steps—to appear more educated than I was. I hoped that befriending Dr. Tabb would enable me to continue in this regard.

Mr. Carlyon was warming to his subject. "And with the continuing growth in global trade, can we expect that more and larger vessels will be needed for long distance trade or will there be more faster and handier smaller boats for more local trade, do you think?"

"When the Admiralty took over the Packet Service, it

wasn't a change for the better. It's nearly brought the traditional Packet boats to an end. I think by next year there will
only be six left in Falmouth. There's talk of the mails being
contracted to private companies operating bigger and more
comfortable ships than the Admiralty and carrying cargo and
passengers," the Captain responded. "You know how travel
and the post have grown with people moving overseas and
what not. However, you may not have heard of the recent
mandate to move to steamships for carrying the mails. Passengers like the idea of not having to rely on the vagaries of
the wind." He took a long draw from his pipe.

I found that I enjoyed listening to the intricacies of the ship
building business more than I thought and I had questions of
my own about trade, passengers and regular commercial
routes; but also about the difficulties, such as with navigation,
storms, and the large numbers of wrecks with lost cargo and
loss of life on the Cornish shores.

William, it seemed, also had questions along those same
lines. "How can we make our vessels stronger and better?
That is, what changes might need to be made that could give
us an advantage over other builders?"

Captain Phillips thought for a moment, his brows knitted
together. I noticed how neatly his white cravat was tied and
how its clean whiteness contrasted against the dark blue of his
jacket. I imagined that his ship was equally neat, sharp, and
orderly. "Although the Packet boats have nearly all gone, the
need for accommodations for passengers is on the rise out of
Falmouth. I think we can all agree on that. And as the crews
and their officers of often still have their own—er, private af-
fairs on the side given the low wages, despite laws against

that," he looked around our circle with a knowing glance, "it would seem to me that having compartments that are convenient, shall we say, for stowing smaller and more valuable articles, would be an advantage, as well." The Captain raised his eyebrows and nodded his head.

"I see," William said. "So, having compartments that are 'convenient' as you say and away from prying excisemen's eyes—and perhaps even more importantly hidden away from pirates or privateers—would be a benefit?"

"Yes, exactly!" Captain Phillips exclaimed, taking a puff of his pipe. "Piracy remains a problem, even now, and not only far away in the China seas. So, I would add that provision for which would mark you out as well." Captain Phillips mused.

"Guns," William stated in concentration, his eyes narrowing.

"Exactly so." Captain Phillips nodded.

I began to feel glad that William was not yearning to be a sailor himself, only to build the vessels as a means of commerce. Not only did seamen have to worry about rocks and weather but being shot at by other vessels was another thing entirely!

"Where are you planning to locate your ship building business, Mr. Carlyon? In Bristol?" Captain Phillips asked, turning toward Charles.

"An excellent and relevant question, Captain Phillips. One that I would like your opinion about. On the one hand, Bristol has the advantage for ship building and many a fine company is there. There's the Floating Harbour, as well as the new quayyard with Hilhouse and Sons, William Ross, Hill and the rest. Several iron works, too, if we decided to go in that direction."

The Captain nodded his head, listening.

"But, in my view, the builders are quite crowded, unless you consider several that are getting on in years. Some, like Williams, may be interested in selling. Perhaps we should use the limited capital we have to buy out an existing establishment, such as Williams, who has been in business since 1817 and has a place of prominence near Canon's Marsh. I did discuss this possibility with Mr. Williams and another company owned by Mr. Guppy. Both want exorbitant prices, of course," Mr. Carlyon smiled and put his pipe back between his teeth with a *clack*.

"Of course," laughed Captain Phillips. "Build versus buy. The age-old question."

"Now, I am also considering Padstow as an option. Padstow produces many a fine ship on the Camel river, as you know, and since it is a smaller town than Bristol, it may be more amenable to our way of life. But then again, it has a much smaller trade, but growing," Charles added in contemplation.

Captain Phillips nodded. "Yes, yes. Padstow is a fine choice as well. However, when you consider the growing size of merchant ships, the kind of vessel that you might be mostly asked for, might I suggest Falmouth instead? Plenty of opportunities there, where our own berth is. We could introduce you to the owner of our ship, and certainly others, if you like. Most passengers wish to go to places where there is a postal service which provides private companies with extra revenue at little cost, you see. Another feather in Falmouth's cap."

"Very generous of you. I have heard only good things

about Falmouth and I will seriously consider your offer. Let me discuss it with Anne and William. I would hope to give you our thoughts before you depart," Mr. Carlyon said, reaching out to shake the Captain's hand.

Falmouth! That must be forty miles from here! On the east side of the peninsula. If William moves there, would I want to move there as well? And Mother? And Anne? Baby Will? My mind was a tumult of emotions that I made sure my exterior barely portrayed. The reality was, we were all going to have to leave Port Quin. I knew that. But to leave the only home I had ever known felt like uprooting the foundations of my entire existence.

I had stolen glances at William during this conversation, wondering what was on his mind. The thought of the distance that might now separate us weighed heavily on my heart, with our love newly formed and only just solidified. I was very aware of my place in this world, where a woman's opinions were rarely sought and even less given due consideration. I wondered how my fate would change if the contents of the Paymaster's box were truly to become mine.

If they were not mine, my fate would be like that of a ship cast adrift, at the mercy of the winds and currents, bound to follow the course charted by whoever would find and have me. If the contents were mine, then I was the captain of my ship and more in control over my destiny, at least to some extent. I couldn't buy property or make decisions without a husband, but I was certainly a more attractive proposition than a penniless fisherman's orphan. I was determined to navigate this sea change with as much grace and strength as I could muster. I began to feel a powerful surge flow through me, and an idea began to develop in my mind. An idea that came to me as a whole fish, so to speak, and with each passing minute, it reinforced my determination to find happiness, even amidst the uncertain winds of change.

"Effy, I hope all this talk of the ship building business isn't boring you too badly," Mr. Carlyon asked, kindly, breaking me from my own thoughts of how I could find future happiness. The wet nurse came to take Will from me for his feeding.

"No, oddly enough I find it all very interesting. I hope you don't think me cheeky, but could I ask a question please?"

"By all means, Effy. Please do," he said, surprised at my sudden interest.

"Well then, with all your ideas and knowledge, wouldn't you rather build your own business rather than buy someone else's?" I offered in a serious tone. "After all, the work you have already done is so very good, it seems to me you are well on your way."

One of Mr. Carlyon's eyebrows raised up. A smile crept over his tanned and wrinkled face. "Effy, I think you have a head for business!" he exclaimed.

Chapter Twenty-Six

BREATHLESS

PORT QUIN, CORNWALL, U.K.

SEPTEMBER 4, 1841

We all dined together that evening and had what was a most charming supper hosted by both Charles and Anne, who was feeling well enough to join us. I found I had grown very fond of Captain Phillips, Dr. Tabb, and Charles in quite a short time and felt I would miss them all as our time together drew closer to an end. Captain Phillips said the winds continued to be unfavourable for his return to London, which was a common problem, but my good fortune and why he was still at our table. I found myself deep in thought, watching them laugh and converse around the table, as one big happy family would, I imagined, although I had never experienced it firsthand.

Mother eyed me curiously. "Effy, I know that wistful look in your eye," she whispered to me. "Ye have grown quite fond of our hosts and their guests."

"Yes, I have. And I shall miss them. That is, I wonder…" My mind was busy putting together fragments of prospects and situations that lay before me into a map. The treasure. Mother. The components of a shipping business. Captain Phillips and his knowledge. Charles and his ambitions. William and how he had hold of my heartstrings. Baby Will. How could I put all these pieces together to continue happy suppers such as these? My mind mapped the pieces together as stepping-stones across a stream, leading to another world. A world I desperately wanted.

William leaned over to me and said, "You seem very quiet this evening. Is your neck pain bothering you?"

I turned to him and said, "What? I mean, no. My neck is not too bothersome. However, I have something I would like to discuss with you, and it is time for me to show you the contents of the paymaster's box. Do you have the key to the workshop?"

"Why yes, I do. I am eager to see it, of course. After supper, allow me," he said.

For the remainder of the meal, I pondered what I would say to him and how.

⟫⟫⟫ ⟪⟪⟪

I couldn't wait to be inside the workshop again. The tar smell tinged with wood shavings, the ink on paper, and the precision of the drafting tools all inspired me to no end. I looked around the room in admiration. William went inside the small adjacent room with his lantern and bent down, opened the locked cupboard and pulled out the paymaster's box.

"To think your mother almost lost her life over this," I remarked, sadly, as he placed the box on the main worktable. I stroked the top of the ancient box.

"My mother is truly courageous," he nodded. "Or perhaps foolish. I often think I would have preferred her to give him something, anything, just to be rid of him."

"He might have done the same thing regardless. She would never betray your future," I said, looking up at him.

"Or yours. The contents belong to you, not me," William stressed. We sat on the wooden bench at the table.

William opened the box at my urging and we both stared at the contents in awe. William's fingers slid over the brilliant gems, and he whispered, "Incredible! I could never have imagined! Each piece must be worth a fortune!" He lifted an amethyst pendant and it shone in the dim light. He set it gingerly down and then lifted the piece wrapped in cloth.

"What is this one?" he asked.

"Open it," I replied, my hands clasped in excitement.

He pulled out the gold filigree cross that I had held with his mother just days before. "Lo and behold! What treasure is this?" He exclaimed.

"Your mother says she believes that stone there to be a yellow diamond because it was wrapped in a leather pouch separately from the other jewels. She thinks it is the most precious piece in the box." I added. We sat adoring its splendor when suddenly, he rewrapped the piece, dropped it back in its place in the box, and snapped the lid shut.

"It's too beautiful. Never in my life! That is, I don't know what to do with it! A piece like that is priceless! I believe it is fearsome."

"I absolutely agree." I echoed.

"When I held it, I felt..I don't know...I felt greed, I am ashamed to say. Greed." William looked at me very confused. "I have never felt such greed in my life."

I put my hand on his arm. "A natural reaction, to be sure. The cross's beauty is overpowering." William nodded.

"But I have thought of a plan using the treasure that I would like to discuss with you. A plan for how to use this treasure for our mutual happiness without evil, or at least my hope is to minimize any evil."

"Go on, I'm listening," William said.

"My plan is this. We will take passage with Captain Phillips to take us onboard the *Charles Tucker* to London—which I believe is the next voyage—with the purpose being to conduct some financial trading business there. We tell him nothing of the exact nature of the treasure. Mother may come as chaperone. We tell your father that I have never been there and that we fancy a trip to the big city as your mother has mentioned how magical it is. When there, we ask the Captain for the best place to trade some of the gems for cash and then immediately put the cash in a reputable bank. Would you trust the Captain to do this?"

"I trust him with my life and have done so already, so yes," William replied. "Is there more to the plan?"

"Yes. We keep the remainder of the gems in a safer place than your home. Perhaps another bank in London."

"Yes, I think I can see the value in that part of the plan." He nodded. "But the Gold Cross, should we keep that piece in a bank nearby?" William wondered.

I looked at him in earnest. "I don't know. Who could we

trust with it? Perhaps we should ask your mother or Captain Phillips, but in a general way?"

"Right. We would need to figure this all out. Go on," William said.

I continued. "I will then ask the Captain to ask the bank to write a bank note—or whatever they call it—to give to your father *anonymously* to start the ship building business in Falmouth or wherever he decides is the best location." William's mouth dropped open. "Yes, I have learned a little bit about money from Mr. Kellow."

"No, I am not surprised by your knowledge. You would do that?" he asked, stupefied.

"Yes, of course I would. But I must remain anonymous as the source of the funding to everyone other than you," I said, firmly, my arms folded tightly in my lap. "This assumes that your father doesn't know about the paymaster's box or its contents. Does he?" I asked.

William replied quickly. "He knows about the coins and the box, but he doesn't know about the contents of the box. Mother and I agreed on this. We didn't want to lie to him but agreed we needed to talk to you first before telling him anything about what was inside. And I didn't even know what the box contained myself, so Mother thought it best to keep it to ourselves for now, especially since we have visitors in the house. But why? Why would you want to keep the source of the money from him? From the rest of the family?"

I nodded at his explanation of what his father knew about the paymaster's box. "Because money changes people. I have seen how money causes ill will and bad feelings. Causes good people to do bad things. And I value them too much for that to happen. You have just seen what one sight of the gold cross did to you! We will say it came from a wealthy banking customer who knew about his search for capital."

"I do see your point, and I believe your plan is a good one. But I too have a condition," he said, firmly, his eyes not leaving mine.

"Oh, what is that?" I asked, glad that a mutually favorable plan was taking shape.

"My condition is that you, anonymously, would become a partner in the shipping venture," he replied, assuming I would know what that entailed.

"And what would that entail, please, if I wanted to remain unknown?" I asked, hesitantly.

"I believe there are different types of partners so that when profits come out of the business, you, as the investor, take a designated share of the profits for yourself in return for taking the risk of making your investment. Do you see?" he asked, trying to explain the term as plainly as he knew it himself.

"I think I understand. Is this something I can keep secret and then stop if I so desire at some point?" I wondered aloud.

William shrugged his shoulders. "I assume so, yes. We can ask questions of the Captain and the bankers when the time comes. Do you accept my condition if I accept yours?"

"Yes, I do." I said, in agreement, sighing with satisfaction.

"I can't help but feel that we should go back to the site—where we found the box. See if there is anything more to be found. You know, see if there is a pot for that lid," he said, with a nod of his head in the direction of a pile of papers being held down by the little tea pot lid with the gold top, now being used as a paper weight apparently. William had a gleam in his eye that told me he was determined to see what more could be found. But I was uneasy about this idea.

I took his hand and interrupted the wheels of scheming that I could see gathering motion in his mind. I explained to him, "I adore that tea pot lid. To me, it is beautiful and humble at the same time, making it precious and special. It sits there happily doing its new duty independently and fearlessly, asking for nothing more. Frankly, out of everything, I would hate to lose it, and I hope it doesn't end up carelessly on the floor in pieces. So, might we not be best to leave well enough alone? Might the lid represent enough of a treasure in and of itself, seeing all that we have found already?" I didn't sound convincing, even to myself.

"Maybe. But what if...? I can't think of leaving Port Quin if I don't at least have one more look out there. The thought gnaws at me. What if there is really more treasure to be found? I already have a plan of you and I together rowing out with a set of tools and..."

"But what if we are seen? I am not sure this would be a good idea and yet I don't want you to go out alone and I don't want to tell others about any of it either." I was in a quandary. "Let's think about this further. But William, there is something exceedingly important that I need to explain to you just as you have explained Will and your past to me."

I tried to order my thoughts in some kind of logical way but to do so seemed impossible. I looked about the room, hoping that revealing my inner demons would not destroy all that I had gained with William.

"I have thought to explain this to you before but couldn't quite bring myself to tell you about my..." I hesitated.

"Your what?" William coaxed.

I sat before him in an ardent turmoil, teetering on the precipice of my disclosure. He looked at me innocently and I was about to break that innocence forever. Drawing a deep breath, I said, "My peculiarity that I have inherited from my Gran. That is, my ability to…" I hesitated again.

"Speak freely, Effy. I have done so with you, completely," he said, giving me his undivided attention.

"Here, in your workshop, your artistry and abilities shape the vessels of your dreams and aspirations. I too have an ability that is very unusual and peculiar," I confessed. My words were delicately laced with both fear and adoration for him. My eyes darted around the workshop, my gaze fell upon the ships in various stages of completion, each a testament to the Carlyons' craft and vision. I continued, gaining strength in my own inner self. "I have inherited the power of foresight, visions of the future that come to me like the whispers of the wind across the open sea. I can't predict when they will come or exactly what they mean. I can't control them and I am embarrassed by it all. Please don't speak to anyone other than your mother about this. I told her as she and I were desperate to find you and I felt I had to tell her."

William's brow furrowed. He drew nearer to me, and his strong presence was a solace to me. "Tell me, my love, of these visions."

My fingers traced the grain of the wood on the table, my words imbued with the ethereal essence of my gift. "I saw the coming of the horrific storm and the fury of it and how it threatened to consume all we hold dear. I didn't understand what they meant at the time or I would have warned the men not to go out that day. During the storm, in the chaos, I went to Kellan Head and I heard your voice beseeching Cade, 'Hand me that board,' trying to save your life and unknowingly setting in motion the tragic course of events that have followed since. I saw the seamen down at the bottom of the sea."

I felt a weight lifted from me as I was finally able to tell him all of my visions. My eyes glistened and my heart ached in the remembrance of the calamity. "I glimpsed the lifeless forms of sailors intertwined with sea kelp. Their cries and screams haunt me still. I have also gained a form of intelligence from my Gran that I can't explain or control. The first time I held the Gold Cross, I saw…" I couldn't go on.

William's eyes softened and he reached out to clasp my hand, a steadying presence amidst the storm of my emotions. "Effy, my love," he spoke, his voice a ray of sun on my troubled mind, "your visions may seem outlandish to some, but to me they are threads woven into the tapestry of who you are. They are part of a beacon of wonder of you, that include this extraordinary gift."

"But this is not all. I have also seen ghosts. The ghosts of my father and his crew. Several times they came to me, urging me to revenge them by killing Cade for his treacherous acts against you during the storm."

"How bizarre and frightening!" William exclaimed.

"Yes, it was terrifying. I had to fight against the urge to turn to their darkness and hatred. Gran helped me with her incantations to use the light to do good. Cade's death was an accident. I only meant to capture him, not kill him. I hope that the ghosts have gone to another realm now that all has been resolved…But I still feel terrible guilt for Cade's accident…" I drifted off.

William put his finger to my lips. "Shhh, my love. I believe you and let's hope the ghosts are gone now. I know Cade's death was exactly that, an accident."

Tears shimmered in my eyes as I continued, "Yet I have also seen promises. When I held the golden filigree cross from the paymaster's box, I glimpsed the promise of happiness, our lives," I said, pointing to him and then to me, "joined together like the beams of a sturdy ship. We embark from this very workshop where our dreams are made from the very vessels you build."

William took a deep breath. "I want you to know this. Your visions may foretell either triumphs or trials. Lately, I have the most peculiar feeling that time moves differently now. Faster now than it did before the storm, making me feel that time is more urgent, more precious than ever. It is as if I can feel time moving, slipping away from me, making me focus on what is most important. Which leads me to say this, perhaps sooner than you might expect. Effy, come what may, I choose to navigate my future with you, hand in hand, forever bound by a love that defies anything."

He drew me into a tender embrace, where I felt alive in his strong arms. More alive than I thought possible and my pain, both physical and mental, melted away. "May I...? That is, I want to..." His voice was hoarse with want and need.

"Yes." I reached for him. I wanted him with my entire body and soul. He was the embodiment of strength, integrity, and charm, his eyes reflecting the depth of his affection for me as he gazed into my soul. I felt myself surrendering to the irresistible pull that I had felt for him the moment we met. Our fingers interlocked and a flame burned through my body, igniting a fire in my loins. The shop around me blurred into insignificance and I was intoxicated with his allure.

He caressed me tenderly as he first traced the curve of my cheeks and then my shoulders with a firm but light touch that sent shivers of delight down my spine. Our breaths mingled, warm and eager, as we leaned closer, our lips hovering just inches apart. In that moment, time stood still, the universe held its breath in anticipation of the imminent combining of our souls. And then, as if guided by fate itself, our lips finally met in a fervent union.

Our pent-up desire and longing spoke of a love that had been quietly burning between us, waiting to spark and ignite. The kiss was an expression of the deep emotions that surged between us. He held me close, pulling me into a locked embrace that melded us together with his strong arms and I surrendered willingly, lost in the intensity of the connection we shared. The heat of our bodies and the tang of the closed shop created tingling sensations. With intensity building, our tongues met in a sensual dance, exploring each other in a hunger that could not be requited. A soft moan escaped my lips as opened my bodice and he kissed lower on the skin on my chest. I didn't want the exquisite sensations of our entwined bodies and hearts beating as one to end.

At last, he pulled back, his forehead touching mine as we caught our breath. He held me by the shoulders and our eyes locked, sparkling with our newfound intimacy, both of us breathless. In that moment, we both knew that our hearts had found our home and that this kiss was only the beginning of a love and a bonding of bodies that would last through eternity.

He looked at me with profound happiness in his eyes.

Breathless, he said, "I have one more question for you, my love. Will you do me the honour of becoming my wife?"

Chapter Twenty-Seven

SOARING SOULS

PORT QUIN, CORNWALL, U.K.

OCTOBER 4, 1841

As William and I stood before the ancient altar of St. Minver's Church, our loved ones by our side, our souls soared. Mr. Kellow, our dear long-time friend, gave me away and Melly, my stalwart friend, was my bridesmaid. Mr. Carlyon and Henry stood by William's side, acting as the part of the best man. I wore my best frock and William, a new jersey, trousers, and black shoes. I felt Mother's and Anne's gazes supporting me from their seats in the front pew. Baby Will Pengelly Carlyon, as he had been christened, lay in Mother's arms, sucking quietly on her thumb. My aunts wiped tears from their eyes with lace handkerchiefs. Captain Phillips and Dr. Tabb had returned to attend our ceremony and celebration. Our peaceful little family was as one and it was the greatest happiness I had ever known.

The ceremony at the church with its sacred rituals and whispered vows, performed by Parson Hockings, unfolded like a dream. William, Mother, and I agreed we could have no one else to conduct the service. His deep voice resonated in my heart and filled it with hope. My eyes never strayed from William's, and in those moments, all I could see was him. The man I had chosen had thankfully chosen me in return. I could feel his devotion pouring from his eyes into mine and I felt a fountain of joy surging through me.

The humble church set amid the moors and perched atop the green hills of Cornwall had witnessed countless generations of love stories, but today, it bore witness to ours. The stone walls, etched with centuries of history, cradled our solemn promises, and the soft glow of sunlight filtered through the stained-glass windows, casting a rainbow of colours upon the worn slate floor and worn pews. Away beyond the church's threshold, the whispering cliffs that guarded Port Quin held their own silent ceremony. Seagulls, like heavenly messengers, circled above, their beautiful wings contrasted against the white billowing clouds just above them. The breeze, fragrant with its briny scent of the sea, carried with it blessings for us, it seemed. From the gulls' view, dark blue lapis water lapped the shore in a foamy fringe and faded into jade coloured green in a glorious display of the artistry of nature. All the elements of earth, sea and sky seemed to rejoice in the love found and sealed between William and me.

The scene shifted later as we made our grand entrance at a wedding feast held at the Carlyons' home. The applause and cheers surrounded us like a warm embrace. We sat at long, rustic cliffside tables adorned with wildflowers and candles.

The guests, our dearest friends and family, had gathered for a lively celebration, long needed after the deadly storm. Their laughter and cheerful chatter filled the air as they raised their glasses in heartfelt toasts to our future happiness. Charles Carlyon gave a traditional toast:

"Here's to the bridegroom and the bride,

May they stick to each other's side.

I hope their life will be of joy,

And that the fust will be a boy."

Which was received with roars of laughter and stamping of feet. Some of the guests brought their fiddles and played lively jigs that infused the air with delightful rhythms. Anne brought out poppy blackberry syrups, sweet-drink mead, and peppermint water, of her own distilling, for those who liked them. Several of the younger people struck up a jig. My brothers followed, making fire fly from the heels of their boots and all the company were quickly whirling without much order.

Throughout the evening, I stole moments to look at William, our hands finding each other's under the table or in the crowd. We reveled in the joy of our loved ones' company and our hearts overflowed with gratitude. Our love had built up over time, like a beautiful pearl, and had fully come to light only after the storm. Our union pivoted on a key moment in time that changed everything that was to come, as the powerful joyful and enduring testament of a painful hardship that would be long remembered. I turned to William at a quiet moment and asked him, "Do you think folks here will see our union as part of the circle of life? That is, a sign that life will go on?"

He smiled at me from his chair, his arms relaxed and

outstretched as he surveyed the crowd. "Many, including those not here tonight, still see me as an outsider. That rubs salt in the wound of Cade's death. Nothing I can do will ever change that or take away the heartbreak of the storm. But as unions like ours form, they bring light back into people's hearts. That is, I hope our union will."

William then took the opportunity to whisk me away to one of the empty cottages nearby which had been provided temporarily for us. The cottage had been abandoned by the prior occupants who moved away from Port Quin very soon after the storm. I knew them but did not know them well. "Let's be away, then," he whispered, taking my hand.

"They're off! They're off!" Several voices cried from behind us, back in the dining room. "Come on before we are too late and they have locked the door!"

William and I ran hand in hand, laughing, the short distance from the Carlyons' house to the small two-story white-washed cottage which seemed the distance of at least a mile away, that's how impatient we both were. Fortunately, the full moon lit up the sky like a beacon and we clearly saw the way. But the mad crowd behind us also saw us very clearly and beat us there. When we went inside, I noticed someone, probably Mother, had placed a vase of purple flowers and a platter of food on the small dining table. I could hear that the well-wishers were already upstairs in the one and only bedroom, sniggering, ready to perform the age-old ritual of "tanning" the married couple to bed, without which they would meet with bad luck all their days. I had been assured by my mother and aunts that this tanning was only for play and that no actual hurtful tanning would occur. When we peered into the bedroom, I wasn't so sure by the wild-eyed look of the crowd surrounding the bed.

"Come in!" they shouted. We went in and laid ourselves on the bed with our clothes on and the wedding guests, panting and out of air, pounded the bed and bedstead with their fists.

"Commence to beatin'!" My brother Richard shouted, with a wild and playful look in his eyes. "First one hit betokens the sex of their first-born!" With that, the guests took their stockings, straps, braces, or anything they could get their hands on and began beating us.

"Give them the pepper!" Henry shouted with glee. "I saw the first strap hit William—boy!" he yelled.

"Give it to 'em boys!" Mr. Carlyon cried out. They continued while William wrapped his arms around my head to protect me and he wailed in protest, "Give us a rest!"

"Very well. Let us go back for all the good wishes are dealt," Mr. Carlyon announced. They rushed away down stairs with great commotion and as they left, we could hear that Henry added, "Make sure you touch the lintel over the hearth with your head for more good luck!"

William and I flopped back on the bed. "Have they really gone?" I asked. "Please shut all the windows and lock the doors," I added in exasperation.

William got up to do as I beckoned but turned his head to look at me, grinning. "Stay here, exactly as you are, and I will be back directly."

I was only too happy to relax for the first time in what seemed like ages, with all the wedding planning and preparations. I laid on my back on the soft downy bed. I would not have to imagine for much longer what William's skin would feel like against mine. Within mere moments, my imaginations and dreams would become reality and I was excited in anticipation as the seconds wound down. Soon, I would have him as mine.

William slowly pushed the door open and entered the room. "All unwanted party guests are gone and all the doors and windows are firmly shut," he assured me. "We are alone at last." He looked at me, smiling, gauging my readiness for what would come next. He slowly took off his coat, his eyes never leaving mine, and he tossed it carelessly on a chair next to the window.

I stretched out my arms to him, my eyes full of want. He laid down on me and kissed me fervently, and my strong calloused hands made quick work of the buttons on his waistcoat, which he wrangled off. He rolled us over on his back and put his hands in my hair, pulling out the pins and tossing them on the bedside table. My hair fell about my shoulders and to my waist and shone in the dim candlelight.

"You know the first time I knew I loved you?" William asked.

"When?" I replied stroking his face with my right hand while I laid half on him and rested on my left side.

"When you came to Henry's aid that day…the day we first arrived here and he cut his knee. Your hair shone in the sun and your kindness shone out like the moon does tonight. I will never forget that day when I first saw you," he whispered and touched my face gently. Then he took my hands in his and stood me up and spun me around to unlace my dress in the back and my bodice, which dropped to the floor in turn. He held me close from behind and his large hands roved up and down my thin shift which he slowly peeled off. I heard him moan and his trousers hit the floor. I turned to him and the full naked skin of our bodies touched for the first time, on fire. He lifted me easily back onto the bed, pulling down the coverlets with one hand and easing us into the sheets with his strong body. He stroked my hair and then the full outline of my body, kissing me fully, and I did the same. His muscles were taut under his skin. I wanted to absorb every inch of him at once. I was surprised at how strong his thighs were and how easily they pushed mine open. Our hands were roving wildly and he took mine to his manhood, which I was very curious about. He toyed with me for what seemed like hours before we could finally wait no longer. Our aching was finally satiated in the act of interlocking. We reveled in becoming one, body and soul. I found my body reverberating like ripples in a pond afterward. Together, we had found what seemed like a new kind of cave in that cottage, one where I would never have to be cold and afraid again.

As we lay ensconced in the embrace of the tranquil night, my senses were heightened and alert. As this was our first night together and our first in this cottage and even though I knew it was only a temporary lodging for us, being there felt strange. What things happened here with its former inhabitants? What were the various creaks and moans I heard as the wind caressed the timbers in its roof? I could hear the distant rhythmic sound of the sea waves which provided something of a soothing backdrop, while the gentle night breeze painted a delicate cool brushstroke across my skin through the open window.

By my side, William lay in a solid slumber, his sound breaths as deep as the night. But the faint rustle of leaves outside our window made me wonder if, despite the serenity of the night, animals lurked about. A rabbit perhaps. A fox or a wild pony searching for food. I couldn't help but have the sense that something was close by, waiting and watching, and it cast a shadow over our newfound happiness. I stayed alert, listening. I crept out of bed and pulled a robe out of my valise that had been placed here prior to my arrival. I thrust my arms in it as I furtively glanced out the window. I sat in the chair by the window, uneasy.

Within a short while, the first glimmers of dawn were breaking and my senses became even more alarmed. I felt another's heartbeat hovering, other than William's. I was anxious and afraid.

"Wiliam. William, wake up. Someone is here." I shook his shoulder.

He sprang up to a seated position on the bed. "Whaaat? What's that you say?" He grumbled, only half awake, his hair pointing in every direction.

"Shhh," I whispered, holding my finger over my lips. "Someone is lurking nearby. I can sense his heartbeat. Someone who means us harm," I warned, as I sat across from him on the bed, cross legged.

His first sleepy reaction was to look at me with questioning, half-closed eyes. But then they suddenly flew open, as if he had suddenly remembered my special gifts. He mouthed, "Quietly. Go downstairs and find a candlestick or a frying pan. Make no sound. I will look out through the windows." I nodded my head. We both pulled on a minimal amount of clothes avoiding the window.

My heart raced with fear. I went down the stairs as bravely as I could, barely touching them and, with my back against the wall, I crept into the kitchen, grabbed a frying pan, and headed back towards the front door. I saw William silently come down the staircase and he nodded his head toward the front door and pointed toward the wall next to it where I should stand. He stood firm with his shirt open, biting his lower lip as he took the doorknob and quickly pulled the door open with all his might. I came round and stood behind William, frying pan at the ready. There, standing in the doorway at his full height was Jack Rowe. His shirt, open at the neck, was stained and wrinkled. His trousers had holes in the knees and his face was unshaven. He said not a word but scowled at William.

"What do you want, Jack?" William spat out.

"I heard the tannin' 'e got last night, though I wasna' invited," he sneered. His face looked gaunt, as if he hadn't eaten well for days. "I heard it all. All the moaning and carryin' on too." The thought that Jack Rowe had heard our most tender moments together sickened me to my core. *What kind of man would stay outside a newly married couple's cottage all night?*

"What of it?" William said brusquely.

"Thought I would wait 'ere to give 'e a tannin' of me own," Jack said in a menacing tone, bearing his yellow and crooked teeth like a snarling stray dog.

"Be gone, Jack. We have no quarrel with you," William said as he quickly began to shut the door. Jack stuck his leg out and put his dirty black boot in the door with a *thud* to block William from closing it.

"But *I* have a quarrel wi' *you*," Jack said in a mocking voice.

"See, it should be Cade 'ere. He wanted the gurl. An' somehow ye two," he stuck a grubby finger out pointing it at William and then at me, "put him at the bottom of a gug. Seems strange to me."

"Get the hell out before I call the alarm." William said.

"Cade said ye had treasure. And I seed ye and the gurl haulin' a black box. Seed it with me own eyes," Jack growled.

"Did you, now? Then you saw us carry a box full of sand. My mother collects boxes. Now, be gone I said." William snorted. He turned away from Jack and tried to push the door closed.

Jack would not be put off so easily. He leaned into the doorway. "Me tanning be this. Wha' yourn can be mine. I tell 'e. Cade lived through the storm an all to be killed off by ye! I be his revenge. I can call another inquest on his death. An' wha's more, I want the treasure. The maid, Hannah said she seed the black box," Jack seethed, his breath reeked. "How can 'e afford a wedding party while the rest of us starve? Eh? I know 'e've got it. I'll 'ave none of yourn lyin' 'bout it!"

William leaned more heavily on the door, which creaked and crackled under the struggle as Jack pushed back with his shoulder and all his body weight. With his other arm, he whipped out a knife and pointed it in my direction. "Give me a part of the treasure, or I swear on Cade's grave the gurl gets it like her sweet 'lil goat." Sweat poured down his neck. Desperation oozed out of his every pore.

William let out a string of profanities. "Enough!" I yelled. "Enough!" Startled for an instant at my outburst, the men paused and looked up. I turned to the dining table and laid the frying pan on it. I grabbed a large tray full of food that my mother and aunts had left for William and me to eat during our stay at the cottage. With only a few steps, I turned back and thrust the tray in the door and jammed it in between the door and frame.

I barked out. "We are not unsympathetic. Jack, you look like you haven't eaten in days. Take it. Take it and go." I pushed the tray forcefully into his hands. Slices of beef, ham, salted pilchards, bread, saffron buns, cheese, butter, apples—enough food for a week—teetered in the balance. Jack's eyes popped open and instinctively he dropped the knife and took hold of the tray. William pushed the side of the tray closest to him through the door, which pushed the whole of Jack backwards, stumbling, out of the doorway. William quickly bent down, scooped up the knife, and tossed it back into the cottage behind us.

"Go." I said, in disgust.

"Leave and never be back here again, you black worm," William added, slamming the door, and locking it. "First time I have seen food used as a weapon. Excellent notion, Effy!" William panted, reaching for my hand. As Jack stumbled away, we watched through the small window. With the tray under one arm, Jack turned and drew his thumb across his throat with an evil cutting gesture, one eye closed for emphasis.

I shivered at his gesture and clenched my other fist. I had the feeling one has of missing the bottom step and losing one's balance, lurching forward, and tumbling down, out of control onto the pavement and hitting it with a heavy, dizzying *thwack*. "So, he knew about the paymaster's box. Did he tell Cade, do you think? Is that why Cade insisted there was a treasure, came here, nearly murdered your mother, and almost murdered me?"

William looked at me dumbfounded. "This. This is why we can't go back to the treasure site. His eyes are on our every move. He tracks us like a starving dog...he senses the jewels somehow. To try to find more treasure now would be the death of you. I can't allow that, as your wife. Do you not see that?" I said, shaking.

"Yes, I see that now," William said, alarmed, his eyes following Jack as he carried the food away from the house.

William and I looked at each other. The threat that loomed at our doorstep was now an undeniable and ugly part of our journey and we knew it. Our love, already tested and tempered by the storm and shadows that had encircled us, now faced this warning of what might lie ahead. His threat was clear and bore down on us with an unsettling weight. An ominous reminder of his watchful eye and relentless desire, his words had marked us like a bad stain on the first chapter of the beautiful, magical story that was our new life together.

Chapter Twenty-Eight

The Story I Told Myself

Port Quin, Cornwall, U.K.

October 5, 1841

And so, my story twisted and turned from hopeless to hopeful, just as the wind, a relentless force, twists, and howls through the crevices of the gray cliffs, carrying with it the echoes of forgotten sorrowful screams and resounding voices. Shouts of seafarers lost to the treacherous depths mingled with the haunting cries of seagulls screeching overhead in a melancholic song of those indomitable spirits who called Port Quin their home.

In what was one of my last moments standing in my family's place of origin, standing on Kellan Head of Port Quin for one last time before I started my journey for London and then for Falmouth, I felt as though I had stepped through a world suspended between the realms of the living and the dead, real and magical. I was in a place where the boundaries of reality and imagination were blurred, where the mysteries of the brooding sea intertwined with the longing of the heart and the inspiration of the mind to form tales of hope, strength, love, and loss, like mine.

Please join me in Book 2 of the *Hopeless Dawn* Series…

Everyone Her Own Tale

SAMPLE EXCERPT

PORT QUIN, CORNWALL, U.K.

OCTOBER 5, 1841

"I don't feel safe here now. Not after Jack Rowe held a knife to our throats!" I exclaimed to William, reaching out for his hands. "We can't stay here! What if he comes back…and brings others!" And the morning after our wedding night! I tried to control my voice but I felt like sobbing.

"I quite agree. No telling what that maniac will do. Besides, we have no food left," William said, teasing me gently. "Good move on your part to shove our wedding week feast platter into his gut to drive him back out the door." He pulled me into his loving embrace and rocked me from side to side. "Quickly, let's gather up our things and make haste to my parents' house. We need to change our departure for London and leave immediately and in complete secrecy."

"Yes, do you think that Captain Phillips can depart earlier than planned?" I looked up at him, concerned.

"Probably." He stroked my disheveled hair. As it was still very early in the morning, we had had no time to properly wash or dress before we had to combat Jack Rowe at the door to the cottage we were allowed to use on our wedding night. He seemed willing to stop at nothing to find and take the treasure we had found just weeks ago off Kellan Head.

I set my jaw in determination. "I have been thinking about the jewels and how to disguise them for our journey to London to deposit them properly in the Bank of London. What if the ship is boarded and searched during the voyage?" I asked, pulling out of William's embrace.

"I share your concern. Pirates or even Duty Officers are real threats. What do you have in mind? Clearly, any kind of chest is a true giveaway," William agreed.

"Unless the chest is completely ordinary. That is why I'm thinking of hiding the jewels in plain sight," I replied as we quickly climbed the stairs to the bedroom. I turned to William behind me and continued. "You remember, like the story of the barrels of butter on the ship that sunk in the parish in 1807 that might have held the paymaster's chest. I bet the jewels were on that butter shipment! Any new bride would certainly be carrying household wares or gifts for a new household. Bed Linens. Crockery. What if we used a small crate or even the paymaster's box with the lock on it and put cutlery on the top layer?"

I sat at the little chair in front of a faded mirror and stroked my hair quickly with a brush. I would be only too happy to depart our temporary cottage arranged for our wedding night, given Jack's attack. We would have to travel far to escape his threat of retribution on the accident that killed his best friend, Cade, who had almost killed me. I shuddered as I remembered the sight of Cade falling helplessly into the pit to his death. Obviously, Jack blamed William and I. William poured water into the basin and slapped a few handfuls on his face. "Hmmm. A bit risky…" He trailed off in thought.

I turned to look at him as I created three sections in my hair, weaving them into a long braid, very glad that William was now mine as my handsome and strong new husband. He was pulling up his trousers over his long, muscular legs as he surveyed the front of the house for intruders out the window. My cheeks reddened as I remembered our torrid union from last night. I was now a very educated married woman. I cleared my throat and continued. "I would say that it is a box of cutlery and no one would be the wiser. Who would question or want to examine a box of old spoons and forks?"

A Hopeless Dawn (1888)

Noted as one of Frank Bramley's finest works, this somber painting immediately pulls at the heartstrings of its audience. Many of the details of the painting are designed to create an emotional response from the viewer. In my opinion, one of the first details that strikes the eye is the pale-yellow light that comes in from the window that hits the window casing, table, and floor, showing the viewer that this is a humble home, a cottage with a meal left uneaten. Then the viewer's eye follows the light toward the shadows of the painting towards the right corner to see more of the story unfold—there you see Bramley's main characters. A beautiful and bereft young woman so distraught that she is kneeling on the cold stone floor and laying in the arms of an elderly women. Her limp hand hangs over an enormous open Bible. The interpretation of her limp hand over the Bible is said to make a link between the two sides of the painting, despair on the left with the uneaten meal on the table and Christian salvation on the right (Jacqueline Banerjee, 2021). The scene is quite moving with the elderly woman's wrinkled hand and caring face trying to comfort the younger one despite what must be a terrible and mutual loss. One could interpret the younger woman as so distraught as to be too disheartened and too weary to have the energy to take any comfort or belief from the Bible despite the older woman's attempts.

According to the gallery label of May 2007, the painting's title "comes from a passage by John Ruskin's *The Harbours of England*, which affirms that "Christ is at the helm of every boat." The implication is that although the bereft wife, whose husband has failed to return from the sea, is being comforted by her mother-in-law, there is a still greater source of comfort: "the open Bible, the altar-like table, and the religious print on the wall hint at the consolations of religion."

A Hopeless Dawn, by Frank Bramley, RA (1857-1915). Oil on canvas. Support: 1226 x 1676 mm (4' x 5.5'); frame: 1595 x 2055 x 145 mm. Collection: Tate, presented by the Trustees of the Chantrey Bequest in 1888. Reference: N01627.

About The Artist

A HOPELESS DAWN (1888)
— FRANK BRAMLEY —

Born on May 6, 1857, in Sibsey, near Boston, Lincolnshire (GRO), he studied at the Lincoln School of Art and Antwerp Academy and spent a year in Venice before arriving in Newlyn at the urging of Walter Langley during the winter of 1884. He spent eleven years at the artists' colony in Newlyn, Cornwall, near the port. The Newlyn School became known for its en plein air scenes, which were so popular at the time and painting in particular what would have been described as long, gentle moods of grey of actual Cornish life. Bramley combined social realism with the new practice of painting outdoors, trying to balance aesthetic concerns with the dramatic narrative so popular amongst Victorians who had a great fondness for heart-rending sentimentalism and a fixation with social class.

Before the 1850s it is interesting to note that Newlyn was an isolated area because of its geographical inaccessibility and the community was very small, but the opening of the railway in 1852 and Brunel's bridge at Saltash in 1859 gave Newlyn a chance to bring more people into its shore. Although artists had visited Cornwall frequently throughout the earlier 19th century and were also lingering in other Cornish towns like St. Ives, it was not until 1882 when Walter Langley, followed by Edwin Harris and then William Wainwright a year later moved to Newlyn. Harris, Wainwright, and Bramley had been friends at Veriat's academy in Antwerp and they suggested that Bramley come to Newlyn in 1886. Bramley had been living in Venice but had been forced to leave because the harsh winters were bad for his health. Bramley sought a close community of artists similar to the one he had in Venice. His friend urged him to move to Newlyn where he stayed in rooms on the top floor of a small cottage on the corner of Bellevue Street in Newlyn. Bramley's tiny, thatched studio was comprised of a small working space and an even smaller room for sleeping above a grocery shop run by a Mrs. Barrett who had lost both arms in an accident who combined her landlord and shop keeper roles with that of guardian of an army of noisy children. Somehow, under these trying circumstances, Bramley was able to create beautiful works, to the admiration of his fellow artists. "All the Newlyn men were industrious and enthusiastic, but Frank Bramley yielded to none either in enthusiasm or industry. Hard work was the rule among the young painters, who, if they did not wholly scorn delights, certainly live laborious days." (Charles Hiatt, "Mr. Frank Bramley, A.R.A., and his Work", in The Magazine of Art, 1901, p 56).

One of the unique techniques Bramley used and that the colony became famous for was the square-brush technique. Bramley was regarded as the chief expert of this technique, which he continued to use well into the 1890s, a time when other artists were abandoning it. The technique is described as follows: An everyday artist, who wants to paint a ship's mast against the sky, takes a brush with a fine point, and draws it vertically up and down on the canvas in the desired place. However, a Newlyn artist does not do this. He or she uses a squarer brush and gets his mast by a series of horizontal strokes. "...of the practitioners of this technique Mr. Bramley is the easy first; indeed, his strength and dexterity are marvelous. He has been called the Father of the Newlyn School." (R. Jope-Slade, 'The Outsiders," in *Black and White Handbook* to the *Royal Academy and New Gallery*, 1893, p.11).

Bramley married fellow artist Katherine Graham in 1891 and she apparently was the model in several of his works. The couple lived at Orchard Cottage, which at the time was called Belle Vue Cottage, from 1893 to 1897. During the 1890's, Bramley became a leader in impressionism and was elected as an associate to the Royal Academy in 1894. In 1895 they moved to the spa town of Droitwich in the West Midlands and by 1900 they settled at Grasmere in the Lake District.

The moves represented changes in location and changes to his motifs, which went from stern social realism to a drowsy, halo of flowers appearance, for example, in 1894 with *Sleep* and *Delicious Solitude* in 1910 in which his beloved Katherine is thought to be the model for the work. In 1911, he became a full member of the Royal Academy. Bramley died at the age of 58 in Chatford Hill in the Cotswolds, Gloucestershire, in August 1915. According to an honourable obituary in The Times, he was a modest, quiet, sweet gentleman.

Acknowledgements

I strayed and stretched into new genres for this novel, which required more creativity and out-of-the-box thinking for me— and I enjoyed it so much! I wish to thank Pat Balmer, Parish Clerk for St Minver, for his responsiveness to my questions about the legend of Port Quin. Also huge thanks to the librarians at Kresen Kernow for their fine digitization of historic volumes such as John Watts Trevan's book so that they may be revered by people like me. I absolutely loved the intense conversations I have had about these characters and their story with my early MS readers: Rose, Chris, Mary, Gwenn, and Larry. Please be ready for more of the same great fun with the next book in the series!

Di Ann Pitts Hand, my fine arts mentor, graciously took the time to create the incredible original painting you see in the illustrations and I am so thankful for her expertise, friendship, and mentoring. What gifts she has for creating realistic scenes like N.C. Wyeth! I hope we will all get to see more of her work!

My developmental editor, Stacia Pellitier, gave me valuable advice and counsel on this work, finding plot holes and incongruencies, so I thank her for her studious thoughts.

The heavy lifting on editing came from John Dirring, Ph.D., once again, as my historical editor who fixed my Americanisms, anachronisms (tea bags in the 19th century?), and my historical inaccuracies. Without him, this novel would not be nearly as meticulously written as it is. Many thanks to John for his responsiveness, his eagle eyes, and historical expertise across so many topics in the Victorian era.

I thank my family for their patience and support for the hours I dedicated to this work. They are truly precious gifts. Finally, I want to thank you, my readers, for engaging in this special story elaborating my adoration of a masterpiece painting. I hope it entertained and inspired you as much as I intended it to. Please join me as the story continues through additional masterpieces by Frank Bramley and his social realism commentary on the unique, beautiful, tragic, and magical world that is Cornwall.

Resources

Bartlett, John. 1996. *The Ships of North Cornwall. Tabb House.*

Doe, Helen. 2006. *The Maritime History of Cornwall: an Introduction.* Tor Mark.

Harmer, Jeremy. 2020. *The Legend of Port Quin. Lyrics, vocals, guitars, hand harmonium mixed and edited by Jeremy Harmer.*

Port Isaac Myths: Of Medical Men and Myths. Cornish Studies Resources. January 2022.

Provis, Geoff. 2009 *The Fishermen of Port Isaac.* Trefeock Publications.

Provis, Geoff. 2011. *The Seafarers of Port Isaac.* Trefeock Publications.

Tate Museum, London. *A Hopeless Dawn* display caption.

United Kingdom Censuses for 1841 and 1851, accessed through the Cornwall online census project, 2023.

The Cornish Bird. 2022. *Port Quin: The Mystery of The Hopeless Dawn.*

Trevan, John Watts. *A Summary of Memoirs of the Parish of St. Endellion Prior to the Year 1834.* Kresen Kernow.org.uk: document ref. X1126

Trevan, Dr. Frederick. *History of Port Isaac and Port Quin by Dr Frederick Trevan, 1833-1834.* Kresen Kernow.org.uk

About The Author

JILL GEORGE, PH.D. is a historical researcher author, and industrial psychologist who specializes in novels about the Victorian era in London and Cornwall, U.K. She writes to rebalance history, leveraging women's successes and the men who supported—and sometimes tried to undermine or downplay—these successes. She travels frequently to London, Cornwall, and Devon to do hands-on research of each site mentioned in her books. Her next novel, the second in the *Hopeless Dawn* series, will be *Everyone Her Own Tale*, based on the painting of the same name by Frank Bramley. The second book in the series is a continuation of the historical gothic romance thriller of Effy and William Carlyon set in Falmouth in majestic Cornwall, U.K. Jill has also written the American Fiction Award Finalist for historical fiction *Illuminating Darwin: Arabella's Light* (2023), which also received editor's pick awards from Publisher's Weekly and Kirkus, as well as *The Light Among Us: The Elizabeth Carne Story, Cornwall* (2022), both receiving five stars from five reviewers at Readers' Favorites. Many photos of Jill's research trips, interviews, and events are on display on her website: **www.jillgeorgeauthor.com** and you can follow her work in progress on Instagram, TikTok, and Threads **@jillgeorgeauthor**. Come and see! Jill lives in Pittsburgh, Pennsylvania USA with her three teenagers, husband, and many pets.

Additional Questions

1. One of the designs of this novel is that large transfor-
    mations take place over a short amount of time. That is,
    an event can be the catalyst to change many things that
    might have been building up over a long time. Has this
    ever happened to you? Can you find examples of this in
    the novel?

2. What themes did you find in the novel and how do they
    compare to experiences you have in your life today?

3. How is William flawed as a protagonist? Can he over-
    come these flaws?

4. In what ways do the characters resemble the setting in
    Cornwall? How are they similar?

5. Describe Effy's transformation in terms of her feeling
    powerless as a woman and how this changes through-
    out the book. How do you feel about your own power
    as a woman (for women readers)? Would you want to
    improve this if you could? How could you?

6. Jago Pengelly represents a patriarchal type of man. How
    much has this changed over the course of time?

7. Taylor Swift, a popular singer songwriter, often writes
    about situations of women dealing with everyday emo-
    tions in relationships. Can you find the eight Easter
    eggs (clues from Taylor Swift songs) from Taylor Swift
    in this novel?

8. What did you think of Effy's mother, Mary, and her role in the family? What impact did she have on the family dynamics?

9. Do you believe in premonitions or being sensitive to events that actually happen in the future? Why or why not?

10. How do legends add to our appreciation of the history of a culture?

11. If you were to write a story about the characters in a masterpiece work of art, which would it be and what would your story entail?

12. How do you interpret the scene in the painting *A Hopeless Dawn*? What do you think of Frank Bramley's use of light in the painting and what do you think he intended it to mean?

Additional Books by Jill George

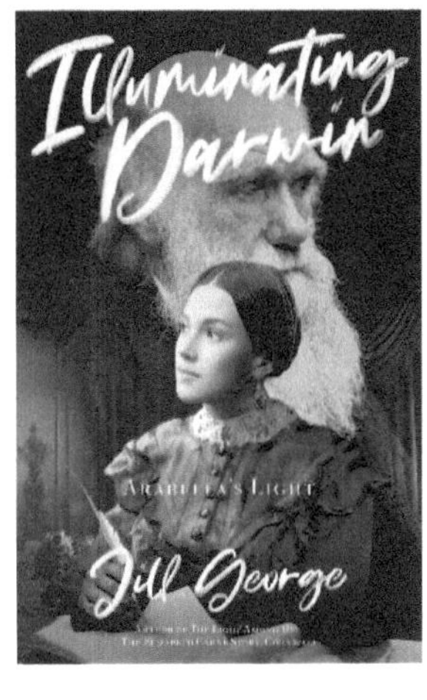

"Heady drama...the story of a woman engaging with ideas that are shaking the world..."

– PUBLISHER'S WEEKLY EDITOR'S PICK

"George's strength lies in immersing the reader in 19th-century England with rich descriptions in natural, first-person narration."

– KIRKUS GET IT ACCOLADE

"A masterpiece of historical writing, Illuminating Darwin by Jill George accomplishes everything a good historical novel should. She illuminates the brilliant, progressive, and determined Arabella Buckley, a woman at the forefront of discovery. Through witty dialogue, informed prose, and emotional depth, George brings history to life in the way only a well-crafted historical novel can…Well worth any reader's time."

– COLIN MUSTFUL, FOUNDER & EDITOR, HISTORY THROUGH FICTION

"Elizabeth Carne was clearly a remarkable woman whose contribution to Cornish society, geology, and the world of banking and commerce has been admirably woven into the well-researched historical novel. It is a story which truly needed to be told...*I could not put this excellent read and fascinating story down*!"

– Tony Mansell, Editor of The Cornish Story

"In her debut novel, George brings forward the home-educated Cornish daughter of a prominent Land's End mining family. Elizabeth C. T. Carne emerges as an unforgettable and challenging character in 19th-century social history. How surprising that most of the main issues of her time still ring true...An excellent and inspiring read!"

– Melissa Hardie, Director, The Hypatia Trust and Women in Words